# ClaSsMateS 1

## Steven J. Molinsky • Bill Bliss

### Ann Kennedy • Gloria Palacios • George Spanos • Robin Thompson

PRENTICE HALL REGENTS
A VIACOM COMPANY
Upper Saddle River, New Jersey 07458

Publisher: *Tina Carver*
Director of Production and Manufacturing: *Aliza Greenblatt*
Editorial Production/Design Manager: *Paul Belfanti*
Production Supervision and Composition: *Paula Williams* and *Ken Liao*
Electronic Art and Realia: *Todd Ware, Marita Froimson,* and *Don Kilcoyne*
Editorial Supervision and Permissions: *Janet Johnston*
Production Coordinator: *Dave Dickey*
Cover Coordinator: *Wanda España*
Photo Researchers: *Teri Stratford* and *Sherry Cohen*
Project Coordinator: *Ann Kennedy*
Career Profiler Researcher: *Marian Hughes*
Pre-formatter: *Rose Ann Merrey*

Interior Design: *Kenny Beck*; *Brian Kobberger, Bill Smith Studios*
Cover: *Bill Smith Studios*
Illustration, page 6: *Richard Hill*

Photographs: *Paul Tañedo*

Special thanks to the students and faculty at Annandale High School.

© 1996 by Prentice Hall Regents
Prentice-Hall, Inc.
A Viacom Company
Upper Saddle River, New Jersey 07458

Printed in the United States of America

10  9  8  7  6  5  4  3  2  1      02  01  00  99  98  97  96

ISBN 0-13-350000-4

Prentice-Hall International (UK) Limited, *London*
Prentice-Hall of Australia Pty. Limited, *Sydney*
Prentice-Hall Canada Inc., *Toronto*
Prentice-Hall Hispanoamericana, S.A., *Mexico*
Prentice-Hall of India Private Limited, *New Delhi*
Prentice-Hall of Japan, Inc., *Tokyo*
Simon & Schuster Asia Pte. Ltd., *Singapore*
Editora Prentice-Hall do Brasil, Ltda., *Rio de Janeiro*

## Acknowledgments

The editors have made every effort to trace the ownership of all copyrighted material and express regret in advance for any error
or omission. After notification of an oversight, they will include proper acknowledgment in future printings.

41  (left) *Yellow Bird* by Frané Lessac/ William Morrow
Publishers
(right) *Looking Along Broadway Towards Grace Church*
by Red Groomes, 1981. From *Red Groomes, a
Retrospective, 1956–1984* (Philadelphia: Pennsylvania
Academy of the Fine Arts, 1985). Reprinted with
permission of the publisher.

57  (mid left) Thomas Kitchin/Tom Stack & Associates
(mid right) Minneapolis Convention and Visitors Bureau

65  (top left) Paul Leibhardt
(top middle) Charles Philip/West Light
(top right) United Nations
(bottom left) Patrick Aventurier/Gamma-Liaison, Inc.
(bottom middle) United Nations
(bottom right) Will & Deni McIntyre/Tony Stone Images

88  (American wedding) Page Poore-Kidder
(Indian wedding) United Nations

(African wedding) Pascal Maitre/Odyssey: Matrix
International

93  From *The New Kid on the Block* by Jack Prelutsky.
Copyright © 1984 by Jack Prelutsky. Reprinted by
permission of Greenwillow Books, a division of William
Morrow and Company, Inc.

94  (top left) Tom and Dee McCarthy/The Stock Market
(bottom right) Rockefeller Folk Art Center

106  (top left) Harvey Lloyd/The Stock Market
(top right) Luc Novovitch/Gamma-Liaison, Inc.
(bottom left) Alain Evrard/Gamma-Liaison, Inc.
(bottom right) Jacques Jangoux/Tony Stone Images

114  Bowling Green State University

123  Neal Peters Collection

128  U.S. Immigration and Naturalization Service

130  AP/Wide World Photos

# Classmates 1 Contents

## School Rules 97

## Registration 103

## Health and Illness 109

## Student Responsibilities 117

# CLASSMATES 1 SUBJECT MATTER STRANDS

## SOCIAL STUDIES

## MATH

## LANGUAGE ARTS

## READING

## WRITING

## JOURNAL WRITING

## FINE ARTS

## RESEARCH

## CAREER PROFILES

# Greetings and Introductions

*In* this chapter, we will cover the following topics and skills:

## SCHOOL COMMUNICATION
➤ Greeting people
➤ Introducing yourself
➤ Introducing others

## SOCIAL STUDIES
➤ Names, titles, and nicknames

## MATH
➤ Using numbers
➤ Using a combination lock

## READING & WRITING
➤ Writing a paragraph
➤ Journal entry: Writing a poem

## COMMUNICATION TIP
➤ Saying you don't understand

## CAREER PROFILE
➤ School secretary

## ASSESSMENT
➤ Self-assessment checklist

**Julia and Anna are meeting for the first time. What are they saying to each other?**

**Fernando is a new student at Gardner High School. Fernando and his mother and father are talking with the secretary in the school office. What are they saying to each other?**

# New Friends

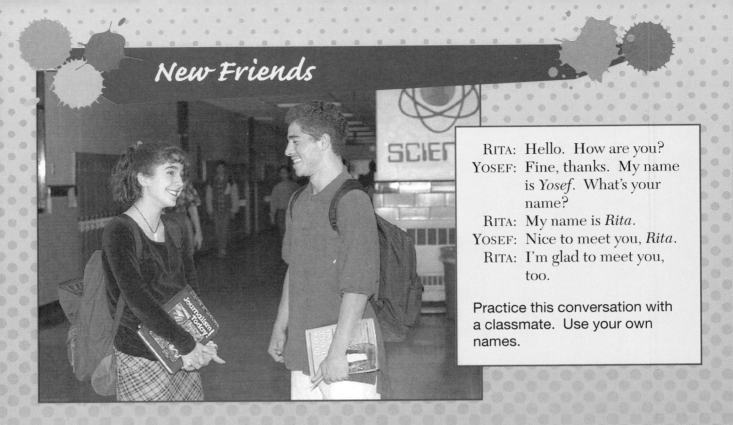

RITA: Hello. How are you?

YOSEF: Fine, thanks. My name is *Yosef*. What's your name?

RITA: My name is *Rita*.

YOSEF: Nice to meet you, *Rita*.

RITA: I'm glad to meet you, too.

Practice this conversation with a classmate. Use your own names.

# A New Student

MRS. CLARK: What's your name?

TERESA: My name is *Teresa Sandoval*.

MRS. CLARK: How do you spell your last name?

TERESA: *S-A-N-D-O-V-A-L*.

MRS. CLARK: What's your address?

TERESA: My address is *315 Green Street*.

MRS. CLARK: What's your phone number?

TERESA: My phone number is *358-2201*.

MRS. CLARK: Where are you from?

TERESA: I'm from *El Salvador*.

MRS. CLARK: Welcome to Central High School.

TERESA: Thank you.

Practice this conversation with a classmate. Use your personal information.

# Classmates Exchange

Circulate around the classroom. Ask five classmates these questions. Write about your classmates in the space below.

What's your name?
How do you spell your first name?
How do you spell your last name?
Where are you from?

| | First name: | Last name: | Country: |
|---|---|---|---|
| ❶ | _____ | _____ | _____ |
| ❷ | _____ | _____ | _____ |
| ❸ | _____ | _____ | _____ |
| ❹ | _____ | _____ | _____ |
| ❺ | _____ | _____ | _____ |

## NUMBERS IN OUR CLASS

How many students are in your class? _____
How many countries are they from? _____

Anna is writing about her English class.

# Writing My Classmates

*"My Classmates"*
*There are 20 students in my English class. Elena is from El Salvador.*
*Jean Paul is from Haiti. Bernardo is from Guatemala.*

Write a paragraph about YOUR English class.

Use this title: "My Classmates"
Use this topic sentence: There are _____ students in my English class.

## Reading A Student Information Form

### STUDENT INFORMATION FORM

**Name**

HERNANDEZ      CARLOS      JUAN

Surname      First name      Middle name

**Address**

313      RIVERSIDE STREET      202

House number      Street name      Apartment number

33176

Zip code

MIAMI      FL

City      State

313-28-6411      9/28/83

Social Security Number      Date of Birth

(305) 267-5922

Telephone number

COSTA RICA

M __X__ F _____      Country of Origin

Sex

1. What's the student's last name? _____
2. What's his first name? _____
3. What's his address? _____
4. What's his phone number? _____
5. What's his date of birth? _____
6. What country is he from? _____

## Writing Your Student Information Form

### STUDENT INFORMATION FORM

**Name**

_____ _____ _____

Surname      First name      Middle name

**Address**

_____ _____ _____

House number      Street name      Apartment number

_____ _____ _____

City      State      Zip code

__ / __ / __

_____ _____ Date of Birth

Telephone number      Social Security Number

M _____ F _____ _____

Sex      Country of Origin

# Listening

## PERSONAL INFORMATION

Listen to the question. Circle the best answers.

1. 315 Green Street — (John Sander)
2. Maria Sanchez — 236-9105
3. 22094 — Mexico
4. 44 North 20th Street — 258-9381
5. 356-22-3821 — 762-7539
6. 525-6328 — 23098

## COMMUNICATION TIP

**Saying you don't understand**

A. What's your surname?
B. I'm sorry. I don't understand.
A. What's your last name?
B. Hong.

Practice with a classmate. Use your surnames.

# Classmates Journal

## A Poem About My English Class

*"People, Places, Friends"*
*Many people from many places.*

| | | | |
|---|---|---|---|
| Linda, | Thuy, | Kim, | Roberto, |
| Singh, | Miho, | Veronica, | Jose. |
| Mexico, | Vietnam, | Korea, | El Salvador, |
| India, | Japan, | Honduras, | Bolivia. |

*Many people from many places,*
*And many, many new friends.*

Start a journal in a composition notebook. Your journal is a place for your own writing.

Create a poem about YOUR English class. First, write it here. Then, copy it into your Classmates Journal.

"_____"

*Many people from many places.* } Names

} Countries

*Many people from many places,*
*And many, many new friends.*

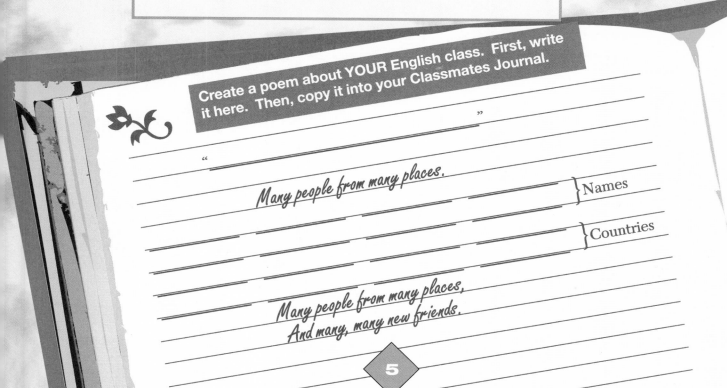

| 1 | one | 11 | eleven | 21 | twenty-one |
|---|-----|----|--------|----|-----------|
| 2 | two | 12 | twelve | 22 | twenty-two |
| 3 | three | 13 | thirteen | 30 | thirty |
| 4 | four | 14 | fourteen | 40 | forty |
| 5 | five | 15 | fifteen | 50 | fifty |
| 6 | six | 16 | sixteen | 60 | sixty |
| 7 | seven | 17 | seventeen | 70 | seventy |
| 8 | eight | 18 | eighteen | 80 | eighty |
| 9 | nine | 19 | nineteen | 90 | ninety |
| 10 | ten | 20 | twenty | 100 | one hundred |

## NUMBERS IN SCHOOL

My locker number is *19*.

My English classroom number is *35*.

My bus number is *24*.

My student number is *7913*.

**What are YOUR numbers at school?**

My locker number is _____.

My English classroom number is _____.

My bus number is _____.

My student number is _____.

My _____ number is _____.

## COMBINATION LOCKS

Write the correct number.

*10*

## USING YOUR COMBINATION LOCK

Practice these instructions for opening a lock.

> 20 - 6 - 32

**1** Right 3 turns.  Stop at *20*.
**2** Left full turn.  Pass 6.  Turn more.  Stop at *6*.
**3** Right to *32*.  Open.

Now give instructions to open locks with these combinations.

> Right 3 turns.  Stop at _____.
> Left full turn.  Pass _____.  Turn more.  Stop at _____.
> Right to _____.  Open.

**1** 10 - 16 - 35
**2** 24 - 4 - 21
**3** 17 - 23 - 4
**4** 8 - 34 - 12
**5** 13 - 15 - 31
**6** 2 - 28 - 18

## WHAT'S THE COMBINATION?

*3*

## WHAT DO YOU CALL THAT?

### Combination Lock

shackle

arrow

knob

numbers

## Names, Titles, and Nicknames

This is Susan.
Her full name is Susan Ann Hawkins.
Her first name is Susan.
Her middle name is Ann.
Her last name is Hawkins.
Her friends call her Sue.
Her mother is Mrs. Hawkins.
Her father is Mr. Hawkins.

This is Ricardo Alejandro Toledo-Claros.
His mother is Mrs. Claros.
His friends call him Ricky.
His father is Dr. Toledo.

This is Hoang.
Her full name is Le Hoang Anh.
Her first name is Hoang.
Her last name is Le.
In her country, Vietnam, her last name comes first.
In the United States, her first name comes first.

## NICKNAMES

> Susan's nickname is Sue.
> Ricardo's nickname is Ricky.

Can you match these names and nicknames?

| | | | |
|---|---|---|---|
| _c_ | ① Michael | a. Johnny |
| ___ | ② Elizabeth | b. Jenny |
| ___ | ③ Thomas | c. Mike |
| ___ | ④ John | d. Bob |
| ___ | ⑤ Katherine | e. Tom |
| ___ | ⑥ Robert | f. Liz |
| ___ | ⑦ Jennifer | g. Kim |
| ___ | ⑧ Kimberly | h. Kathy |

## TITLES

> *Mr.* is a title for a man.
> *Mrs.*, *Ms.*, and *Mrs.* are titles for women.
> *Dr.* is a title for a doctor.

Write the titles and names of five people you know.

❶ _____

❷ _____

❸ _____

❹ _____

❺ _____

# Classmates Exchange

Circulate around the classroom. Ask eight classmates these questions. Write about your classmates in the space below.

> What's your full name?
> What's your nickname at home?
> What's your nickname at school?

| Full name: | Nickname at home: | Nickname at school: |
|---|---|---|
| _____ | _____ | _____ |
| _____ | _____ | _____ |
| _____ | _____ | _____ |
| _____ | _____ | _____ |
| _____ | _____ | _____ |
| _____ | _____ | _____ |

# ClaSSMaTeS
## CAREER PROFILE

## The School Secretary

Joanne McRae
School Secretary

EDUCATION: Executive Secretarial Program

JOB DESCRIPTION: Answer the phone
Type
File
Manage the office

WORK LOCATION: Main office of a high school

QUOTE: "Every day is different!"

## SELF-ASSESSMENT CHECKLIST

### Check It Out!

**I know how to:**

- [ ] greet people
- [ ] introduce myself
- [ ] introduce others
- [ ] give personal information
- [ ] use numbers
- [ ] use a combination lock
- [ ] spell
- [ ] fill out a student information form
- [ ] say I don't understand

**I know about:**

- [ ] different kinds of names
- [ ] different kinds of numbers

**I can write:**

- [ ] a paragraph about my English class
- [ ] a poem about my English class

# School Orientation

## 2

*I*n this chapter, we will cover the following topics and skills:

### SCHOOL COMMUNICATION
➤ Identifying places in school
➤ Identifying school personnel
➤ School supplies

### SOCIAL STUDIES
➤ Nationalities

### MATH
➤ Using money

### READING AND WRITING
➤ Reading prices
➤ Reading and writing a rap
➤ The Writer's Craft: Rhyming

### COMMUNICATION TIP
➤ Asking to borrow something

### CAREER PROFILE
➤ Social Studies Teacher

### ASSESSMENT
➤ Self-assessment checklist

**Who are these people? Where are they?
Can you name other people and places in your school?**

# New Places

**1**  A. <u>Where is he?</u> _____

    B. <u>He's in the</u> _____ classroom.

**2**  A. _____

    B. _____ library.

**3**  A. _____

    B. _____ office.

**4**  A. _____

    B. _____ nurse's office.

**5**  A. _____

    B. _____ gym.

**6**  A. _____

    B. _____ cafeteria.

**7**  A. _____

    B. _____

    auditorium.

**8**  A. _____ you?

    B. I'm _____ .

# A School Interview

MINERVA: Hello. What's your name?
MR. GROVE: My name is *Mr. Grove*.
MINERVA: What's your job?
MR. GROVE: I'm *a P.E. teacher*.
MINERVA: Where do you work in the school?
MR. GROVE: I work in the *gym*.
MINERVA: Thank you.
MR. GROVE: You're welcome.

*a P.E. teacher*
*gym*

**Practice these interviews.
Use names of people in your school.**

**1 the librarian**
library

**2 a guidance counselor**
guidance office

**3 a secretary**
office

**4 a music teacher**
music room

**5 the principal**
office

**6 the nurse**
nurse's office

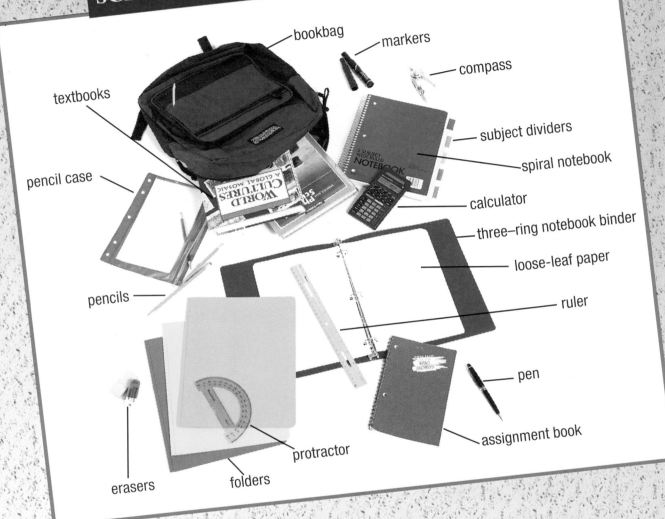

bookbag

markers

compass

textbooks

subject dividers

spiral notebook

pencil case

calculator

three–ring notebook binder

loose-leaf paper

pencils

ruler

pen

protractor

assignment book

erasers

folders

| | |
|---|---|
| three–ring notebook binder | protractor |
| compass | folders |
| ruler | subject dividers |
| pen | markers |
| assignment book | bookbag |
| calculator | pencils |
| erasers | pencil case |
| textbooks | loose-leaf paper |
| notebook paper | spiral notebook |

# Classmates Exchange

Work with a classmate. Check your bookbags.

| School supplies: | You have: | Your classmate has: |
|---|---|---|
| three-ring notebook binder | ☐ | ☐ |
| notebook paper | ☐ | ☐ |
| pencils | ☐ | ☐ |
| eraser | ☐ | ☐ |
| calculator | ☐ | ☐ |
| textbooks | ☐ | ☐ |
| assignment book | ☐ | ☐ |
| subject dividers | ☐ | ☐ |
| pens | ☐ | ☐ |

## ✓ COMMUNICATION TIP

**Asking to Borrow Something**

A. May I borrow a pencil?
B. Sure. Here you are.
A. Thanks.
B. You're welcome.

Practice new conversations with other school supplies.

# Listening

## YOUR SCHOOL SUPPLIES

Listen and write the number on the correct line.

_____

_____

1

_____

_____

_____

_____

_____

15

## Coins

 penny
$.01
1 cent

 nickel
$.05
5 cents

 dime
$.10
10 cents

 quarter
$.25
25 cents

 half dollar
$.50
50 cents

 silver dollar
$1.00
1 dollar

## Currency

(one-)dollar bill
$1.00
1 dollar

five-dollar bill
$5.00
5 dollars

ten-dollar bill
$10.00
10 dollars

twenty-dollar bill
$20.00
20 dollars

## WHAT'S THE AMOUNT?

| 25¢ | $1.25 | 60¢ | $20.50 | $10.20 | $5.60 |
|---|---|---|---|---|---|

1. ___$1.25___

2. _____

3. _____

4. _____

5. _____

6. _____

# How Much Is It?

FABIANA: How much is a *notebook*?
SHOPKEEPER: Two dollars and forty-five cents.

Make up prices for these school supplies.
Then practice conversations with a classmate.

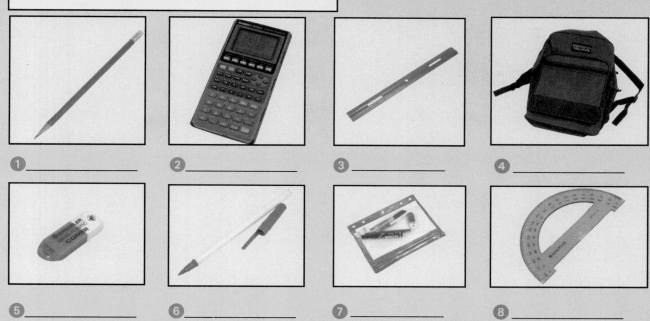

1 _____

2 _____

3 _____

4 _____

5 _____

6 _____

7 _____

8 _____

**CONSUMER AWARENESS**

# COMPARISON SHOPPING

What are the prices of school supplies at two
different stores?

| | Store #1 | Store #2 |
|---|---|---|
| notebook | _____ | _____ |
| bookbag | _____ | _____ |
| calculator | _____ | _____ |
| .................... | .................... | .................... |
| .................... | .................... | .................... |
| .................... | .................... | .................... |

## Classmates Around the World

People study English all around the world.

My name is Manjit.
I'm Indian.
I'm from Delhi.
Delhi is a city in India.
India is in Asia.

My name is Carlos.
I'm Mexican.
I'm from Guadalajara.
Guadalajara is a city in Mexico.
Mexico is in North America.

My name is Luisa.
I'm Italian.
I'm from Rome.
Rome is a city in Italy.
Italy is in Europe.

My name is Karina.
I'm Bolivian.
I'm from La Paz.
La Paz is a city in Bolivia.
Bolivia is in South America.

My name is Muhammad.
I'm Somalian.
I'm from Mogadishu.
Mogadishu is a city in Somalia.
Somalia is in Africa.

My name is Wan.
I'm Chinese.
I'm from Beijing.
Beijing is a city in China.
China is in Asia.

Fill in the chart with the names of these students and the information about them.
Then interview some classmates and make a new chart.

| Name | Nationality | City | Country | Continent |
|------|-------------|------|---------|-----------|
|      |             |      |         |           |
|      |             |      |         |           |
|      |             |      |         |           |
|      |             |      |         |           |
|      |             |      |         |           |
|      |             |      |         |           |

### MAP PRACTICE

**Look at a world map with your classmates.
Can you find different cities and countries?
Can you identify the continents?**

# Classmates Rap

Practice this rap and perform it with your classmates.

## Our International Celebration

We're from England, Finland, Poland, and Spain.
Mozambique, Togo, Zaire, and Bahrain.
I come from Somalia.
She comes from Sudan.
He's from Tunisia.
They're from Japan.
Algeria, Nigeria, Syria, Namibia,
Zambia, The Gambia, Colombia, and Cambodia.
We're from Switzerland, Swaziland, Iceland, and Ireland,
Lithuania, Latvia, Bolivia, and Thailand.
We're different people from different nations.
Come join our international celebration!

### What words rhyme in the rap?

Sudan _____Japan_____      The Gambia _____

Bahrain _____      Iceland _____

Algeria _____      Bolivia _____

Now create a new rap about nationalities.

### THE WRITER'S CRAFT

**Rhyming**
*Japan* and *Sudan* are rhyming words. The ends of these words sound the same. Writers sometimes use rhyming words in poetry and music.

19

## Social Studies Teacher

Susie Matthews
Social Studies Teacher

| | |
|---|---|
| Education: | Bachelor of Science (B.S.) degree in Elementary Education |
| | Graduate school courses in Education and Social Studies |
| JOB DESCRIPTION: | Teach social studies classes |
| | Plan lessons |
| | Evaluate students |
| | Communicate with parents |
| WORK LOCATION: | Classroom |
| QUOTE: | "I help students grow!" |

### SELF-ASSESSMENT CHECKLIST
## Check It Out!

**I know:**
- ☐ places in the school
- ☐ school personnel
- ☐ school supplies
- ☐ coins and money
- ☐ nationalities
- ☐ countries
- ☐ continents

**I know how to:**
- ☐ ask for information
- ☐ ask to borrow something
- ☐ buy school supplies
- ☐ compare prices in different stores
- ☐ give information about my nationality, city, and country

# School Activities

# 3

*I*n this chapter, we will cover the following topics and skills:

**SCHOOL COMMUNICATION**
➤ Daily school activities
➤ Extracurricular activities
➤ Yearbook pictures

**MATH**
➤ Telling time
➤ Ordinal numbers

**FINE ARTS**
➤ Everyday life in art
➤ Sugar Cane by Diego Rivera

**READING AND WRITING**
➤ Reading a bell schedule
➤ Writing a class schedule
➤ The Writing Process: Pre-writing, Organizing ideas, Writing a first draft

**COMMUNICATION TIP**
➤ Reporting late for school

**CAREER PROFILE**
➤ Coach

**ASSESSMENT**
➤ Peer-assessment checklist

**Where are these students? What are they doing?**

# CLASSMATES YEARBOOK

## DAILY LIFE AT SCHOOL

Sandra is getting on the bus.

Rosa is changing classes.

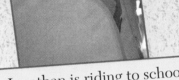

Jonathan is riding to school.

André is having lunch.

Irene is waiting for the bell to ring.

Tuyet is going home.

Mrs. Perez is taking attendance.

With a classmate, practice conversations about these yearbook pictures.

A. What's *Sandra* doing?
B. *She's getting on the bus.*

# EXTRACURRICULAR ACTIVITIES

The students in the Drama Club are practicing for the school play in the auditorium.

The students in the International Club are having a meeting in the cafeteria.

The band is marching on the football field.

The choir is singing in the music room.

Students in the Journalism Club are writing the school newspaper in Mrs. Baxter's classroom.

Volunteers are tutoring children at an elementary school.

The cheerleaders are practicing in the gym.

With a classmate, practice conversations about these yearbook pictures.

A. Where's *the band*?
B. *It's on the football field.*
A. What's *it* doing?
B. *It's marching.*

A. Where are *the cheerleaders*?
B. *They're in the gym.*
A. What are *they* doing?
B. *They're practicing.*

**Analog**

**Digital**

| nine o'clock | nine-oh-five | nine ten | nine thirty |

| 9:00 | nine o'clock |
|------|-------------|
| 9:01 | nine-oh-one |
| 9:02 | nine-oh-two |
| 9:09 | nine-oh-nine |
| • | |
| 9:10 | nine ten |
| 9:11 | nine eleven |
| • | |
| 9:59 | nine fifty-nine |
| 10:00 | ten o'clock |

BOB: What time is it?
CARLOS: It's *eleven-oh-eight*.

Practice conversations with a classmate.

 **1**

 **2**

 **3**

 **4**

 **5**

 **6**

 **7**

 **8**

# Ordinal Numbers

## JEFFERSON HIGH SCHOOL
### BELL SCHEDULE

| | |
|---|---|
| 1st period | 7:30–8:20 |
| 2nd period | 8:25–9:11 |
| 3rd period | 9:16–10:02 |
| 4th period | 10:07–10:53 |
| 5th period | 10:58–11:44 |
| Lunch period | 11:49–12:28 |
| 6th period | 12:33–1:19 |
| 7th period | 1:24–2:10 |

| | | | | | |
|---|---|---|---|---|---|
| 1st | first | 5th | fifth | 9th | ninth |
| 2nd | second | 6th | sixth | 10th | tenth |
| 3rd | third | 7th | seventh | 11th | eleventh |
| 4th | fourth | 8th | eighth | 12th | twelfth |

With a classmate, make up questions about the bell schedule at Jefferson High School.

A. What time is *1st* period?
B. *1st* period is from *7:30* to *8:20*.

A. It's *11:17*. What period is it?
B. It's *5th* period.

## ✔ COMMUNICATION TIP

### Reporting Late for School

JUAN: I'm late. Here's a note from my parents.

SCHOOL SECRETARY: Okay. Let' see. What time is it?

JUAN: It's 9:18.

SCHOOL SECRETARY: Go to your 3rd period class.

JUAN: Thank you.

Practice with a classmate. Use different times.

## Listening
### WHAT DO YOU HEAR?

Listen and circle the letter of the word you hear.

1. a. first   b. third
2. a. six   b. sixth
3. a. 2:00   b. 12:00
4. a. 5:02   b. 2:05
5. a. 7:00   b. $7.00
6. a. $4.50   b. $4.15
7. a. 32   b. 23
8. a. 3:30   b. $3.30
9. a. $12.05   b. 12:05
10. a. 11th   b. seventh

## YOUR CLASS SCHEDULE

Write your class schedule in your Classmates Journal. For each period, list the times, the subject, the room number, and your teacher's name.

25

## *Writing* Observe and Record

What's happening right now in your school? What are people doing in all the different places in your school building?

As a class, talk about locations, people, and activities in your school and write the information on this chart.

**THE WRITING PROCESS**

- Pre-writing
- Organizing ideas
- Writing a first draft
- Revising
- Writing a final copy

| Location | People | Activities |
| --- | --- | --- |
| | | |
| | | |
| | | |
| | | |
| | | |

### GET ORGANIZED

Look at the chart. What are you going to write about first? second? third? Organize your ideas.

### WRITE

Write a paragraph about locations, people, and activities in your school.

Use this title: "A Moment in Time at My School." Use this topic sentence: People are doing a lot of things in my school.

**WRITING TIP:** Indent the first sentence of a paragraph.

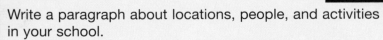

*A Moment in Time at My School*

*People are doing a lot of things in my school.*

# ClassMates  Everyday Life in Art

In the painting on this page, many people are doing many things.

Discuss with your classmates:  Who are the people in this painting?  What are they doing?

Write a paragraph about the painting.

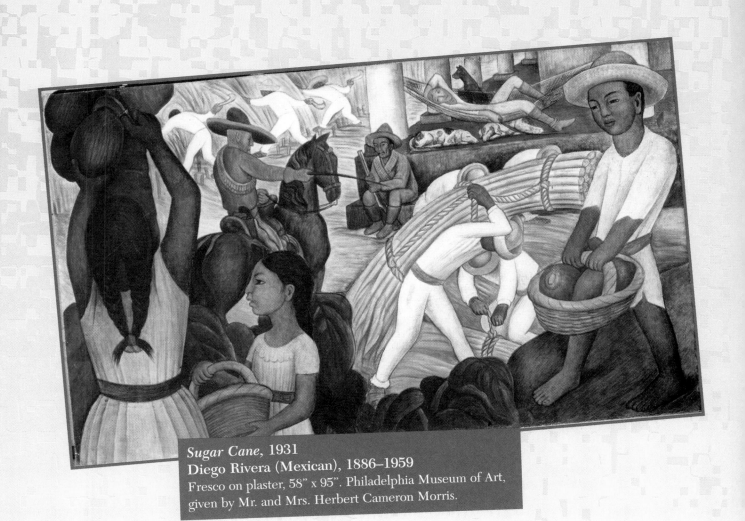

*Sugar Cane*, 1931
**Diego Rivera (Mexican), 1886–1959**
Fresco on plaster, 58" x 95". Philadelphia Museum of Art, given by Mr. and Mrs. Herbert Cameron Morris.

# ClassMates
## CAREER PROFILE

## Coach

Charles W. Hoskins
"Chuck"
Coach

EDUCATION: Bachelor of Arts (B.A.) degree in Psychology and History

Master of Education (M.Ed.) degree

Certificate, Universidad de Valladolid, Spain

JOB DESCRIPTION: Coach football and wrestling

Teach History and Psychology

WORK LOCATION: High school

QUOTE: "I enjoy teenagers. I love to help and watch them develop into successful young adults."

## PEER–ASSESSMENT CHECKLIST
## Check It Out!

My classmate knows:

- ☐ daily school activities
- ☐ extracurricular activities
- ☐ ordinal numbers

My classmate knows how to:

- ☐ tell time
- ☐ read a bell schedule
- ☐ report late for school
- ☐ write a class schedule
- ☐ write about activities in a school, using the writing process
- ☐ describe scenes in paintings

# Classroom Actions

**4**

*I*n this chapter, we will cover the following topics and skills:

**SCHOOL COMMUNICATION**
➤ Classroom activities
➤ Days of the week
➤ Months of the year
➤ Yearbook pictures

**MATH**
➤ Ordinal numbers
➤ The calendar

**SOCIAL STUDIES**
➤ Interpreting bar graphs
➤ Making a bar graph

**READING AND WRITING**
➤ The Writing Process: Pre-writing, Organizing ideas, Writing a first draft

**COMMUNICATION TIP**
➤ Asking the date

**CAREER PROFILE**
➤ School Librarian

**ASSESSMENT**
➤ Self–assessment checklist

**What are the students doing? What are they saying?**

Rosa is sharpening her pencil.

Kevin is erasing his mistake.

Linda and Mai are handing in their homework.

Eddie and Ana are talking to their teacher.

I'm raising my hand.

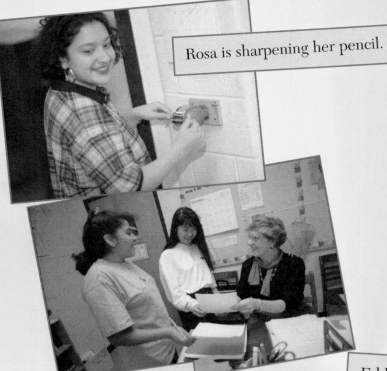

The substitute teacher is writing his name on the board.

My friends and I are opening our books.

With a classmate, practice conversations about these yearbook pictures.

A. What's Rosa doing?
B. She's sharpening **her** pencil.

A. What are Linda and Mai doing?
B. They're handing in **their** homework.

A. What are **you** doing?
B. I'm raising **my** hand.

Pepe is writing in his notebook.

Karen is helping her classmates.

Susan and Michael are checking their answers.

Claudia is reading her poem to the class.

I'm doing my homework.

We're working on our science project.

Lan is doing her homework on the computer.

With a classmate, practice conversations about these yearbook pictures.

A. Is Pepe writing in **his** notebook?
B. Yes, he is.

A. Is Karen doing **he**r homework?
B. No, she isn't.
A. What's she doing?
B. She's helping **her** classmates.

# What Are They Doing?

Fill in the words.  Then practice the conversations with a classmate.

| he | her | his | my | their | they | she | your | you |

**1** A.  What are ___you___ doing?
   B.  I'm doing _____ Math homework.

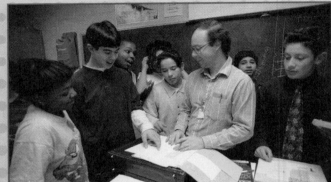

**2** A.  What are _____ doing?
   B.  They're talking to _____ teacher.

**3** A.  What's _____ doing?
   B.  He's writing _____ answer on the board.

**4** A.  What are _____ doing?
   B.  We're using _____ calculators.

**5** A.  What's _____ doing?
   B.  She's writing in _____ notebook.

**6** A.  What am I doing?
   B.  You're teaching _____ wonderful students!

# WHAT'S THE WORD?

| classrooms | cook | her | his | teacher | their | working | writing |
|---|---|---|---|---|---|---|---|

Everybody at Watson High School is _____working_____¹. Mrs. Moore, the school principal, is _____² an important letter. Miss Li, a _____³, is helping _____⁴ students with _____⁵ homework. Mr. Soto, the PE teacher, is playing basketball with _____⁶ students. Mrs. Appleby, the _____⁷, is making lunch. The students are very busy, too. They're studying in their _____⁸.

## Listening
### CLASSROOM ACTIVITIES

Listen and write the number under the correct picture.

_____   _____   ___1___   _____

_____   _____   _____   _____

## Writing   My School Library

Write a paragraph about your school library.

OBSERVE AND RECORD   Visit the school library with your classmates. What's the librarian doing? What are the students doing? Write your observations.

ORGANIZE YOUR IDEAS   Look at your observations. What are you going to write about first? second? third? Organize your ideas.

WRITE A FIRST DRAFT   Write a paragraph about the librarian, students, and activities in your school library. Use this title: "My School Library."

## THE WRITING PROCESS

- Pre-Writing
- Organizing ideas
- Writing a first draft
- Revising
- Writing a final copy

**WRITING TIP:**

Begin your paragraph with a topic sentence. Remember to indent.

| 13th | thirteenth | 20th | twentieth | 40th | fortieth |
| 14th | fourteenth | 21st | twenty-first | 50th | fiftieth |
| 15th | fifteenth | 22nd | twenty-second | 60th | sixtieth |
| 16th | sixteenth | 23rd | twenty-third | 70th | seventieth |
| 17th | seventeenth | • | | 80th | eightieth |
| 18th | eighteenth | • | | 90th | ninetieth |
| 19th | nineteenth | 30th | thirtieth | 100th | one hundredth |

## Practice saying these ordinal numbers.

| 13th | 30th |
| 14th | 40th |
| 15th | 50th |
| 16th | 60th |
| 17th | 70th |
| 18th | 80th |
| 19th | 90th |

### COMMUNICATION TIP

**Asking the date**

A. What's today's date?
B. It's the *16th*.
A. The *16th*?
B. Yes. That's right.

Practice the conversation with a classmate. Use different dates.

## THE CALENDAR AND DAYS OF THE WEEK

| Sunday | Monday | Tuesday | Wednesday | Thursday | Friday | Saturday |
|---|---|---|---|---|---|---|
| | | | 1 | 2 | 3 | 4 |
| 5 | 6 | 7 | 8 | 9 | 10 | 11 |
| 12 | 13 | 14 | 15 | 16 | 17 | 18 |
| 19 | 20 | 21 | 22 | 23 | 24 | 25 |
| 26 | 27 | 28 | 29 | 30 | | |

### DAYS OF THE WEEK

Sunday
Monday
Tuesday
Wednesday
Thursday
Friday
Saturday

With a classmate, practice conversations about the calendar.

A. What day is the *27th*?
B. *Monday*.

A. What dates are on *Thursday*?
B. The *2nd*, the *9th*, the *16th*, the *23rd*, and the *30th*.

| Months of the Year | |
|---|---|
| January | July |
| February | August |
| March | September |
| April | October |
| May | November |
| June | December |

EMILY: When's your birthday?

VANESSA: July 30th. When's YOUR birthday?

EMILY: November 22nd.

Practice the conversation with a classmate. Use your own birthdays.

## BIRTHDAYS IN MR. WILSON'S CLASS

**INTERPRETING BAR GRAPHS**

This is a picture of Mr. Wilson's class. It isn't a photograph of people. It's a picture of information. It's a **graph** of birthdays. Eight birthdays are in January. Two birthdays are in February. How many birthdays are in March? April? May? June? July? August? September? October? November? December?

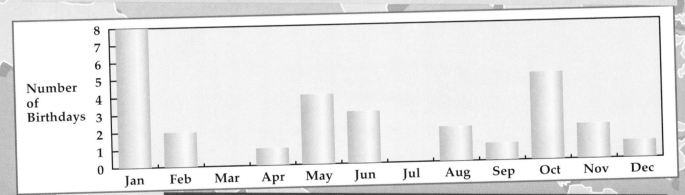

**MAKE A BAR GRAPH**
Ask all your classmates: When's your birthday? Count the number of birthdays in each month. Make a bar graph of birthday information for your class.

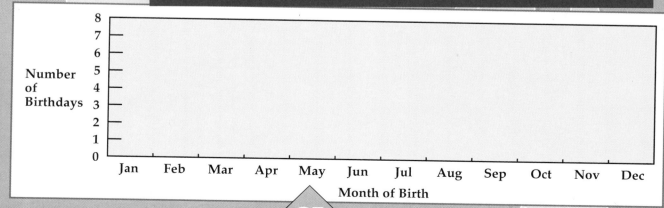

## School Librarian

Mary Herrington
School Librarian

EDUCATION: Bachelor of Arts (B.A.) degree in History

Master of Arts (M.A.) degree in History

Master of Library Science (M.L.S.) degree

JOB DESCRIPTION: Manage the library and hold classes for students

Help students develop an interest in reading

Select books for the library

WORK LOCATION: School library

QUOTE: "I reach children with good literature."

### SELF-ASSESSMENT CHECKLIST
## Check It Out!

**I know:**
- ☐ classroom activities
- ☐ days of the week
- ☐ months of the year
- ☐ ordinal numbers

**I know how to:**
- ☐ ask for the date
- ☐ read a calendar
- ☐ read a bar graph
- ☐ make a bar graph
- ☐ write about my school library using the writing process

# Class Schedules

5

*In* this chapter, we will cover the following topics and skills:

## SCHOOL COMMUNICATION
➤ Names of school subjects
➤ Describing classes and teachers
➤ Class schedules

## INFORMATION SKILLS
➤ Interpreting bar graphs
➤ Making a bar graph

## FINE ARTS
➤ Yellow Bird by Frane Lessac
➤ Looking Along Broadway Towards Grace Church by Red Groomes

## MATH
➤ Fahrenheit and Celsius temperatures

## READING AND WRITING
➤ Journal entry: About school
➤ Reading a class schedule
➤ Reading a letter
➤ Writing a letter

## COMMUNICATION TIP
➤ Asking permission to go to the nurse's office

## CAREER PROFILE
➤ Science teacher

## ASSESSMENT
➤ Self-assessment checklist

**What are these school subjects?**
**Which school subjects are you taking?**
**What's your favorite subject?**

# How Are Your Classes?

RICK:   How's your first day of school going?

JULIA:  Great!  My first period class is Math.  It's a large class, and the students are noisy, but the teacher is very good.

RICK:   My first period class is Science.  The class is small, and the students are very smart.

JULIA:  Who's your Science teacher?

RICK:   I don't know his name.

JULIA:  Is he tall or short?

RICK:   He's tall, and he's very thin.

JULIA:  Oh, that's Mr. Madison.  He's a new teacher.  He's very nice.  Is the class difficult?

RICK:   It isn't difficult, and it isn't easy.  It's interesting.

## Classmates Journal

How's school going for you this year?  How are your classes?  your teachers?  your classmates?  Write your opinions in your Classmates Journal.

# A CLASS SCHEDULE

| PERIOD | CLASS | TEACHER | ROOM |
|--------|-------|---------|------|
| 1st | P.E. | Mr. Razon | the gym |
| 2nd | Mathematics | Mr. Allen | 217 |
| 3rd | English | Ms. Campbell | 115 |
| 4th | Social Studies | Mrs. Jenkins | 208 |
| 5th | Health | Ms. Adler | 126 |
| 6th | Science | Mrs. Perez | 130 |
| 7th | Art | Miss Lee | 105 |

With a classmate, make up questions about this student's class schedule.

A. What's your *third* period class?
B. *English*.

A. Who's your *Health* teacher?
B. Ms. Adler.

A. When's your *P.E.* class?
B. *First* period.

A. Where's your *Social Studies* class?
B. In *Room 208*.

## MRS. CAMPBELL'S HOMEROOM

Use the bar graph to complete the paragraph about Mrs. Campbell's homeroom class.

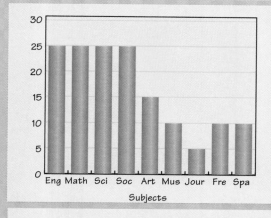

There are 25 students in Mrs. Campbell's homeroom class. Their class schedules are very different. All ___25___ [1] students are taking English, Math, Science, and Social Studies, but _____ [2] students are taking Art, _____ [3] students are taking Music, _____ [4] students are taking Journalism, _____ [5] students are taking French, and _____ [6] students are taking Spanish.

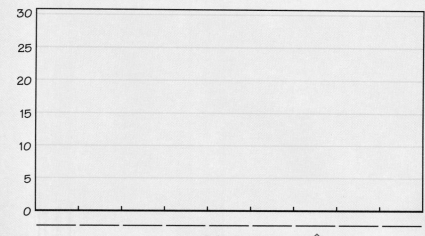

**MAKE A BAR GRAPH:**
**Electives in Our Class Schedules**

How many students in your class are taking English? Social Studies? Science? Math? Art? Music? Spanish? other electives in your school? Count the number of students who are taking different classes. Put the information on the bar graph.

Subjects

# CLASSMATES OPINION SURVEY

Put an *X* on the lines to describe your opinions and feelings about life in school.  Think about reasons for your answers.  As a class, put together the survey information and discuss the results.

## CLASSES

| English | _____ | |
| | *easy* | *difficult* |
| Math | _____ | |
| | *easy* | *difficult* |
| Social Studies | _____ | |
| | *easy* | *difficult* |
| Science | _____ | |
| | *easy* | *difficult* |
| . . . . . . . . | _____ | |
| (Elective) | *easy* | *difficult* |
| . . . . . . . . | _____ | |
| (Elective) | *easy* | *difficult* |

## SCHOOL ACTIVITIES

| Talking with friends | _____ | |
| | *happy* | *sad* |
| Eating lunch | _____ | |
| | *happy* | *sad* |
| Playing sports | _____ | |
| | *happy* | *sad* |
| Doing homework | _____ | |
| | *happy* | *sad* |
| Riding on the bus | _____ | |
| | *happy* | *sad* |
| . . . . . . . . | _____ | |
| (Activity) | *happy* | *sad* |

## SCHOOL PLACES

| Lunch room | _____ | |
| | *quiet* | *noisy* |
| Gym | _____ | |
| | *quiet* | *noisy* |
| Classroom | _____ | |
| | *quiet* | *noisy* |
| Library | _____ | |
| | *quiet* | *noisy* |
| School bus | _____ | |
| | *quiet* | *noisy* |
| . . . . . . . . | _____ | |
| (Place) | *quiet* | *noisy* |

September 7

Dear Lisa,
    I'm in a new school this year. Logan High School is very large. Many students are from different countries. My best friends are from China, Guatemala, and Haiti.
    My new class schedule is great! I'm very busy. I'm taking English, Art, Math, Science, Social Studies, and Dance. I'm also playing in the Orchestra. The work is hard, but I'm very happy! My teachers are very helpful.
    How are you? How are your classes? Tell me about your new teachers and friends.

Your pen pal,
Sara

**Write a letter to a pen pal.**

# ClassMates

### Lessac and Groomes

The places in these two paintings are very different. Life for people in these places is very different. Describe the places you see. What are the artists saying about these places? What's your opinion of these places?

*Yellow Bird*
Frané Lessac

*Looking Along Broadway Towards Grace Church*
Red Groomes.

## WHAT'S THE TEMPERATURE?

A. What's the temperature?
B. It's 37 degrees Fahrenheit/4 degrees Celsius.

Practice conversations with a classmate.
Use the temperatures on these thermometers.

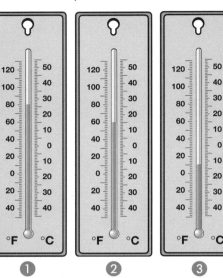
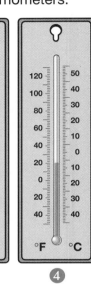

① ② ③ ④

⑤ ⑥ ⑦ ⑧

## WHAT DO YOU CALL THAT?

**Thermometer**

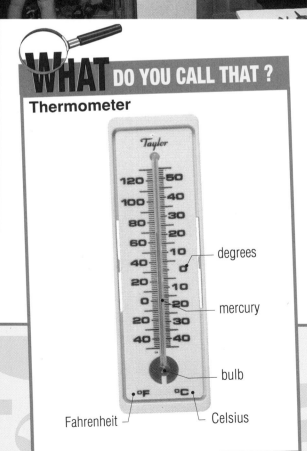

degrees

mercury

bulb

Fahrenheit — Celsius

## FAHRENHEIT OR CELSIUS?

Choose the correct temperature.

1. "It's very cold."              (15° F)        28° C
2. "It's warm."                   20° C          40° F
3. "It's cool today."             85° F          10° C
4. "It's snowing."                15° C          15° F
5. "It's very hot today."         35° C          35° F
6. "There's snow!"                10° F          20° C

## MATCHING

Match the temperatures.

|     |   |       |    |       |
| --- | - | ----- | -- | ----- |
| _d_ | ❶ | 70°F  | a. | 0°C   |
| ___ | ❷ | 32°F  | b. | -16°C |
| ___ | ❸ | 84°F  | c. | 12°C  |
| ___ | ❹ | 9°F   | d. | 21°C  |
| ___ | ❺ | 53°F  | e. | 25°C  |
| ___ | ❻ | 77°F  | f. | 29°C  |

## CELSIUS OR FAHRENHEIT?

Choose the correct temperature.

1. The water is beginning to freeze. It's ( 0°F  (0°C) ).
2. Your temperature is normal. It's ( 98.6°F  98.6°C ).
3. The chicken is cooking at ( 350°F  350°C ).
4. I'm sick. My temperature is ( 39°F  39°C ).
5. It's a warm day. It's ( 35°F  35°C ).
6. The water is boiling. Its temperature is ( 212°F  212°C ).

**COMMUNICATION TIP**

Asking permission to go to the nurse's office

A. May I go to the nurse's office?
B. What's the matter?
A. I feel sick.
B. All right. Go ahead.

A. Are you okay?
B. No. My temperature is *101 degrees Fahrenheit.* I'm going home.
A. I hope you feel better.

**Practice with a classmate. Use different temperatures.**

43

# ClassMates
## CAREER PROFILE

Mrinalini K. Sadananda
Science Teacher

### Science Teacher

EDUCATION: Bachelor of Science (B.S.) degree in Chemistry and Biology

Graduate coursework in science

JOB DESCRIPTION: Teach Chemistry and Biology

Help students with science projects

WORK LOCATION: Science classroom and lab

QUOTE: "Science is never boring. My students are fascinated with science experiments. I especially enjoy doing the experiments with them."

## ANNOUNCEMENTS

Mr. Green's science classes are in different rooms today. Listen and write the correct room number for each period.

| Period | Room | Period | Room |
|--------|------|--------|------|
| 1st | _210_ | 4th | _____ |
| 2nd | _____ | 5th | _____ |
| 3rd | _____ | 6th | _____ |

### SELF-ASSESSMENT CHECKLIST
## Check It Out!

I know:

- [ ] names of school subjects
- [ ] parts of a thermometer
- [ ] different ways of telling temperatures

I know how to:

- [ ] describe my classes and teachers
- [ ] read a class schedule
- [ ] read a bar graph
- [ ] make a bar graph
- [ ] do an opinion survey
- [ ] write a letter to a pen pal
- [ ] describe scenes in paintings
- [ ] read a thermometer
- [ ] use Fahrenheit and Celsius temperature scales
- [ ] ask permission to go to the nurse's office

# Family

**6**

*In this chapter, we will cover the following topics and skills:*

**SCHOOL COMMUNICATION**
➤ Family members

**SOCIAL STUDIES**
➤ Nuclear and extended families

**MATH**
➤ Reading Roman numerals
➤ Writing Roman numerals

**READING AND WRITING**
➤ Journal entry: *Family tree*
➤ The Writing Process: *Pre-writing, Organizing Ideas, Writing a first draft*
➤ Writing a paragraph: *A Moment in Time at Home*

**COMMUNICATION TIP**
➤ Getting someone's attention

**CAREER PROFILE**
➤ Parent teacher liaison

**ASSESSMENT**
➤ Self-assessment checklist

**What family members are in these photos?**

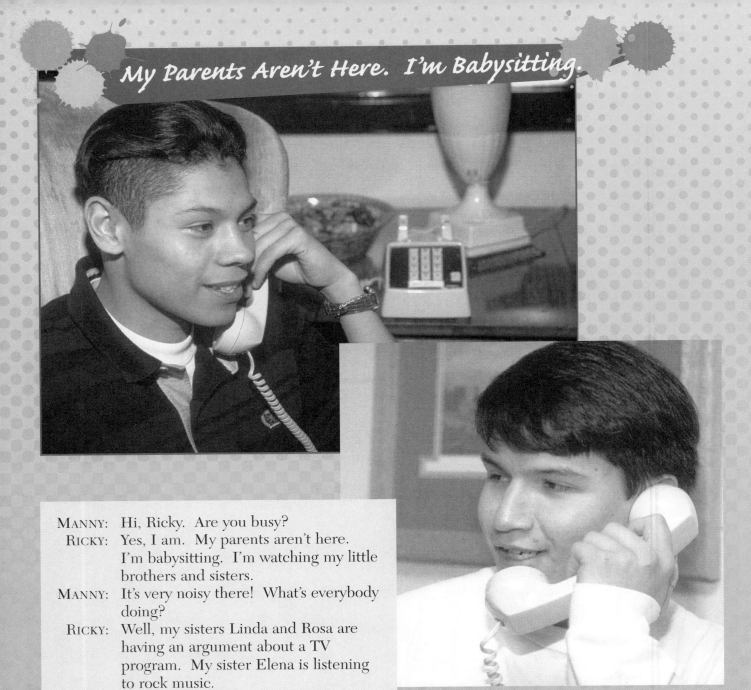

MANNY: Hi, Ricky. Are you busy?

RICKY: Yes, I am. My parents aren't here. I'm babysitting. I'm watching my little brothers and sisters.

MANNY: It's very noisy there! What's everybody doing?

RICKY: Well, my sisters Linda and Rosa are having an argument about a TV program. My sister Elena is listening to rock music.

MANNY: Is somebody playing a musical instrument?

RICKY: Yes. That's my little brother Joey. He's practicing the saxophone.

MANNY: And why is your dog barking?

RICKY: The dog is barking at my brother's saxophone.

MANNY: Where are your parents?

RICKY: My mother and father are eating at a restaurant tonight. It's their wedding anniversary.

MANNY: Well, good luck!

RICKY: Thanks.

Practice this conversation with a classmate. Then create a new conversation: You're calling your classmate on the telephone. It's very noisy at your classmate's home. Ask what's happening.

# A Family Tree

Rosa    Oscar

Natalia    Daniel    Diego    Adriana    Fernando

Flora    Freddy    Catalina    Cynthia

| | | | | |
|---|---|---|---|---|
| cousins | aunt | mother | grandchildren | uncle |
| daughter | husband | son | wife | |

The Serrano family is a big family.  Oscar is Rosa's _____husband_____ [1]. Rosa is the _____ [2] of Daniel, Diego, and Adriana.  Daniel is married.  His _____ [3] is Natalia.  They have two children.  The name of their _____ [4] is Flora, and the name of their _____ [5] is Freddy.  Adriana is Flora and Freddy's _____ [6]. Adriana's _____ [7] is Fernando.  They have two children, too.  The name of their older _____ [8] is Catalina.  The name of their younger _____ [9] is Cynthia. Flora, Freddy, Catalina, and Cynthia are _____ [10]. They are Rosa and Oscar's _____ [11]. Diego is not married.  He's single.  Diego is the _____ [12] of Flora, Freddy, Catalina, and Cynthia.

With a classmate, ask and answer questions about the family tree.  Be sure to give all the information possible about each person!

A. Who is *Daniel*?
B. *Daniel is Rosa and Oscar's son, Natalia's husband, Flora and Freddy's father, Diego and Adriana's brother, and Catalina and Cynthia's uncle.*

## Classmates Journal

### Your Family Tree

Draw your own family tree and write about your family members in your journal.

| | |
|---|---|
| MISS PERRY: | Good morning. Welcome to Madison Intake Center. |
| FRANCO: | Hello. My name is Franco Ruiz. These are my parents, Mr. and Mrs. Ruiz. |
| MISS PERRY: | How do you do? My name is Miss Perry. I'm the registrar. Are you registering your children for school today? |
| FRANCO: | Miss Perry, my parents' English isn't very good. I'm already in school. Today we're registering my brothers and my cousin. |
| MISS PERRY: | Okay. Who's first? |
| FRANCO: | This is my cousin. He's six years old. |
| MISS PERRY: | What's his name? |
| FRANCO: | Jimmy Arenas. |
| MISS PERRY: | Are these people his mother and father? |
| FRANCO: | Yes. This is my aunt, and this is my uncle. |
| MISS PERRY: | What are their names? |
| FRANCO: | Antonio and Marta Arenas. |
| MISS PERRY: | Nice to meet you, Mr. and Mrs. Arenas. And who is this? |
| FRANCO: | This is my brother Eddie. He's seven years old. And this is my brother Rodrigo. He's six years old. |
| MISS PERRY: | It's nice to meet you. |

**Practice this conversation with a classmate. Then create a new conversation. You're enrolling some family members in school.**

## ✔ COMMUNICATION TIP

**Getting someone's attention**

| | |
|---|---|
| ANA: | Excuse me. |
| MS. DAVIS: | Yes? |
| ANA: | Can you help me, please? |
| MS. DAVIS: | Yes. Just a moment. Now, how can I help you? |
| ANA: | My name is Ana Gutierrez. I'm registering for school. |

With a classmate, practice conversations to get someone's attention.

Joy is writing a paragraph about life in her home.
She's using **the writing process**.

- *Pre-writing*
- *Organizing ideas*
- *Writing a first draft*
- Revising
- Writing a final copy

### • Observe and record

me—doing homework

little brother—watching TV

baby—sleeping

sister—reading

big brother—talking on telephone

grandmother—cooking dinner

mom and dad—working

### • Organize ideas

in the living room—little brother

big brother

in the kitchen—grandmother

me

in the bedroom—sister

baby

not home—mom and dad

### • Write a first draft

A Moment in Time at Home

It's a Thursday afternoon in my home. My brothers are in the living room. My little brother is watching TV. My big brother is talking on the telephone. My grandmother and I are in the kitchen. She's cooking dinner and I'm doing my homework. My sister is reading in her bedroom. The baby is sleeping there. My mother and father aren't home. They're working.

## *Writing* A Moment in Time at Home

### Write a paragraph about life in your home.

OBSERVE AND RECORD    You are at home after school. Who's at home? What's each person doing? Write your observations.

ORGANIZE YOUR IDEAS    Look at your observations. What are you going to write about first? second? third? Organize your ideas.

WRITE A FIRST DRAFT    Write a paragraph about the people and activities in your home after school. Use this title: "A Moment in Time at Home."

| | |
|---|---|
| I | 1 |
| V | 5 |
| X | 10 |
| C | 100 |
| D | 500 |
| M | 1000 |

### What are these numbers?

| | | | | | | | | | |
|---|---|---|---|---|---|---|---|---|---|
| I | 1 | VI | 6 | XI | 11 | XX | 20 | LXX | 70 |
| II | 2 | VII | 7 | XII | 12 | XXX | 30 | LXXX | 80 |
| III | 3 | VIII | 8 | XIII | 13 | XL | 40 | XC | 90 |
| IV | 4 | IX | 9 | XIV | 14 | L | 50 | C | 100 |
| V | 5 | X | 10 | XV | 15 | LX | 60 | M | 1000 |

### Matching

| | | | |
|---|---|---|---|
| _c_ | ① XI | a. | 45 |
| ___ | ② XVI | b. | 1150 |
| ___ | ③ XLV | c. | 11 |
| ___ | ④ LXV | d. | 16 |
| ___ | ⑤ MCL | e. | 65 |

### Write the Roman Numerals

① 21 _____

② 55 _____

③ 73 _____

④ 99 _____

⑤ 140 _____

⑥ 1115 _____

### THE ROMAN NUMERAL SYSTEM

II = 1 + 1 = 2          IV = 5 - 1 = 4

VI = 5 + 1 = 6          IX = 10 - 1 = 9

XX = 10 + 10 = 20       XL = 50 - 10 = 40

XVI = 10 + 5 + 1 = 16   XC = 100 - 10 = 90

### MCMXCVIII

| | | | |
|---|---|---|---|
| M | = | 1000 | |
| CM | = | 900 | 1998 |
| XC | = | 90 | |
| VIII | = | 8 | |

### Write these years in arabic numerals.

① MCMXCVI        _1996_

② MCMXCIX        _____

③ MCMLXXXVII     _____

④ MM             _____

⑤ MCMLXXXIX      _____

### Write these years in roman numerals.

① 1997    _MCMXCVII_

② 1983    _____

③ 1978    _____

④ 1917    _____

⑤ 2001    _____

### LISTENING

Listen and circle the number you hear.

| | | |
|---|---|---|
| ① | (VIII) | XVII |
| ② | XXI | XI |
| ③ | XLII | XXII |
| ④ | XLV | XIV |
| ⑤ | CV | CLX |
| ⑥ | LXXXVI | CXXXIV |

### ROMAN NUMERAL SEARCH

Look for roman numerals in your school and community. Write them down, bring them to class, and write them as arabic numerals with your classmates.

# ClassMates

**Nuclear families and extended familes**

The Anderson family is a **nuclear** family. The mother, father, daughter, and son are together in one home. Aunts, uncles, and cousins are living in other places.

The Sanchez family is an **extended** family. Their whole family is together in one home. The mother, father, sons, daughter, and a grandmother are on the first floor. An aunt, an uncle, four cousins, and another grandmother are on the second floor.

**Talk with a classmate. Tell about your family life. Are you part of a nuclear family or an extended family?**

**CRITICAL THINKING**

## What's Your Opinion?

What are some good things about life in each type of family? What are some bad things?

## Parent–Teacher Liaison

Yonnara Keng
Parent-Teacher Liaison

| | |
|---|---|
| Education: | Bachelor of Arts (B.A.) degree in Cambodian Literature |
| | Additional college coursework |
| JOB DESCRIPTION: | Help parents, teachers, and students. |
| | Serve as the bridge between different languages and cultures |
| WORK LOCATION: | School |
| QUOTE: | "I like the work. When I help someone, I go home feeling good." |

### SELF-ASSESSMENT CHECKLIST

## Check It Out!

**I know:**
- [ ] family members
- [ ] roman numerals

**I know how to:**
- [ ] interpret a family tree
- [ ] draw a family tree
- [ ] register family members in school
- [ ] introduce teachers and parents
- [ ] write a paragraph about activities at my home
- [ ] read roman numerals
- [ ] write roman numerals

**I know about:**
- [ ] extended families
- [ ] nuclear families

# The Classroom

*In this chapter, we will cover the following topics and skills:*

**SCHOOL COMMUNICATION**
➤ Classroom objects
➤ Taking an inventory

**SOCIAL STUDIES**
➤ Shopping around the world

**MATH**
➤ Word problems with addition

**READING AND WRITING**
➤ The Writing Process: Pre-writing, Organizing ideas, Writing a first draft

**COMMUNICATION TIP**
➤ Asking what something is called

**CAREER PROFILE**
➤ Math resource teacher

**ASSESSMENT**
➤ Self-assessment checklist

**Where are the students? What are they learning? Can you name the things you see in their classrooms?**

# WHAT DO YOU CALL THAT ?

1. teacher's desk
2. globe
3. file cabinet
4. bulletin board
5. bookshelf
6. computer
7. board
8. eraser
9. chalk
10. chalk tray
11. flag
12. calendar
13. desk
14. textbook
15. wastebasket/trash can

## COMMUNICATION TIP

**Asking what something is called**

A. What's that called?
B. It's *a file cabinet*.

Practice with a classmate. Use the classroom objects on this page.

# Classmates Exchange

Work with a classmate. Ask each other about things in your classroom.

A. Is there a *pencil sharpener* in the classroom?
B. Yes, there is.
A. Is there a *file cabinet* in the classroom?
B. No, there isn't.
A. Are there *bookcases* in the classroom?
B. Yes, there are.
A. Are there *lockers* in the classroom?
B. No, there aren't.

## CLASSROOM OBJECT INVENTORY

Do an inventory of things in your classroom. Count an object, as other students count different objects. Then, circulate around the classroom and ask each other questions. Write the information on the inventory sheet.

A. How many *chairs* are there in the classroom?
B. There are *30 chairs* in the classroom.

A. How many *computers* are there in the classroom?
B. There is *one computer* in the classroom.

A. How many *globes* are there in the classroom?
B. There aren't any *globes* in the classroom.

### Inventory Sheet

| | |
|---|---|
| _____ desk | _____ wastebasket |
| _____ pencil sharpener | _____ thermometer |
| _____ board | _____ fan |
| _____ table | _____ clock |
| _____ dictionary | _____ flag |
| _____ eraser | _____ bulletin board |
| _____ file cabinet | _____ map |
| _____ computer | _____ globe |
| _____ stapler | _____ bookshelf/ |
| _____ chair | bookshelves |

## Writing My Classmates

THE WRITING PROCESS

- *Pre-writing*
- *Organizing ideas*
- *Writing a first draft*
- Revising
- Writing a final copy

Write a paragraph about your classroom.

OBSERVE AND RECORD   What things are there in your classroom? Write your observations.

ORGANIZE YOUR IDEAS   Look at your observations. What are you going to write about first? second? third? Organize your ideas.

WRITE A FIRST DRAFT   Write a paragraph describing the items in your classroom. Use this title: "My Classroom."

# Memory Games

**Disappearing Act!**

**Coverup!**

A. What's missing?

B. . . . . . . . . . . . . . . . . . .

A. $\begin{cases} \text{Right.} \\ \text{Wrong.} \end{cases}$

PLAYERS: Two classmates

MATERIALS: Ten classroom objects

HOW TO PLAY:
Classmate 1 puts ten objects on a desk or table. Classmate 2 studies the objects. Classmate 2 closes his or her eyes, and Classmate 1 hides an object. Classmate 2 looks at the objects and names the missing object.

A. What objects are there on the table?

B. There are *two pencils*. There is *one eraser*. There are *three paper clips*.

PLAYERS: Two classmates

MATERIALS: Different numbers of different classroom objects (for example: 2 pencils, 1 eraser, 3 paper clips) and a cloth

HOW TO PLAY:
Classmate 1 puts the objects on a desk or table. Classmate 2 studies the objects. Classmate 1 covers the objects with a cloth. Classmate 2 guesses the objects and the number of objects.

## *Listening*

### CLASSROOM SOUNDS

Listen and write the number under the correct picture.

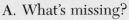

_____

_____

_____

_____

1

_____

These people are shopping in an outdoor market. People are selling things at stands. There are places to buy food, clothes, and other things for the home.

These people are shopping in small stores. The stores are on a street in the center of town. There is a hardware store, and there is a bookstore. There are stores with clothes for men, women, and children.

In the mall, there are big department stores and many small stores. The stores are all together in one big building. There are places to buy many different things. There are also restaurants and movie theaters.

# Classmates Exchange

Tell about shopping in your country. What kinds of places are there to shop? Is there an outdoor market? Are there small stores in the center of town? Is there a shopping mall? Are there department stores?

**CRITICAL THINKING**

# ? What's Your Opinion?

What are good things about outdoor markets? small stores? shopping malls?

## Saying and Solving Addition Problems

$$\begin{array}{r} 9 \\ + 6 \\ \hline 15 \end{array}$$

$$9 + 6 = 15$$

We say: Nine plus six equals fifteen.

**Say the math problems.**

1. $7 + 3 = 10$
2. $5 + 4 = 9$
3. $\begin{array}{r} 11 \\ + 9 \\ \hline 20 \end{array}$
4. $13 + 6 = 19$
5. $\begin{array}{r} 25 \\ + 8 \\ \hline 33 \end{array}$

**Write the math problems two ways and say them.**

1. Four plus three equals seven.

   $4 + 3 = 7$

2. Eight plus nine equals seventeen.

3. Six plus five equals eleven.

$$\begin{array}{r} 4 \\ + 3 \\ \hline 7 \end{array}$$

4. Twenty plus two equals twenty-two.

5. Thirteen plus twelve equals twenty-five.

6. Ten plus four equals fourteen.

## WHAT DO YOU CALL THAT?

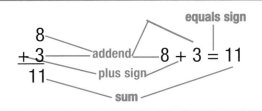

A. What are the addends?
B. *8* and *3*.
A. What's the sum?
B. *11*.
A. How do you say the math problem?
B. *8* plus *3* equals *11*.

With a classmate, practice conversations about addition. Use the math problems in Exercises 1–6 above.

## Ways to Say It!

What's 9 plus 6?
Add 9 and 6.
9 plus 6 equals . . .
What's the sum of 9 and 6?
How much is 9 plus 6?
How much does 9 plus 6 equal?

Practice these different ways to say addition problems. Then work with a classmate. Ask each other easy addition problems and answer them. Try to use all the different ways to say the problems.

## Listening

Write and solve the addition problems you hear.

1. $2 + 8 = 10$
2. _____
3. _____
4. _____
5. _____
6. _____

# Word Problems with Addition

In Mr. Davidson's classroom, there are 28 desks for students and 1 desk for the teacher. How many desks are there in Mr. Davidson's classroom?

$$\begin{array}{r} 28 \\ + 1 \\ \hline 29 \end{array}$$

A. What's the operation?
B. Addition.
A. What are the addends?
B. *28* and *1*.
A. What's the sum?
B. *29.*
A. So what's the answer to the problem?
B. *There are 29 desks in Mr. Davidson's classroom.*

Solve these word problems. Then practice conversations about these problems with a classmate.

1. There are a lot of books in Ms. Winter's bookcase. There are 30 dictionaries on the top shelf. There are 20 textbooks on the bottom shelf. How many books are there in all in Ms. Winter's bookcase?

$$\begin{array}{r} 30 \\ + 20 \\ \hline 50 \end{array}$$

2. There are 18 female students in Mr. Jordan's Math class. There are 13 male students in the class. How many students are in Mr. Jordan's Math class?

3. There are 25 classrooms in the school. In each classroom, there is one wastebasket. There are also one wastebasket in the office and one wastebasket in the library. What's the total number of wastebaskets in the school?

4. There are a lot of things on Roland's desk. There are 12 markers, 2 pens, 3 paper clips, and 1 pencil. How many things are there in all?

5. At Valley High School, there are 121 female students and 105 male students. What's the total number of students at Valley High School?

6. There are 3 computers in the library, 2 computers in the principal's office, 1 computer in the clinic, and 25 computers in the computer lab. What's the total number of computers in the school?

Now make up two original word problems with addition, give them to a classmate, and practice conversations.

## Ways to Say It!

There are 216 students in the school.
There are 216 students *in all.*
The *total number* of students in the school *is* 216.
*There's a total of* 216 students in the school.

Practice these different ways to say sums. Then practice different ways to give the answers to Exercises 1-6 above.

# ClassMates
## CAREER PROFILE

## Math Resource Teacher

Wyllona Evans Harris
Mathematics Resource
Teacher

EDUCATION: Bachelor of Science (B.S.) degree in Mathematics Education

Master of Education (M.Ed.) degree in Mathematics Education

JOB DESCRIPTION: Help in math classrooms

Give students special help in math

Prepare students for tests

Team teach with math teacher

Give math placement tests to new students

WORK LOCATION: High school math classrooms

QUOTE: "I enjoy young people. I want them to see the beauty of Mathematics."

---

### SELF-ASSESSMENT CHECKLIST
## Check It Out!

**I know:**

- ☐ classroom objects
- ☐ different ways of shopping around the world
- ☐ word problems in addition

**I know how to:**

- ☐ ask what things are called
- ☐ take an inventory of things
- ☐ write about my classroom using the writing process
- ☐ describe shopping in different cultures
- ☐ say, write, and solve addition problems
- ☐ solve and talk about word problems with addition

# Clothing

8

**What are the students wearing? What clothes are popular in your school?**

# Is That a New Jacket?

CHARLIE: Alex, is that a new jacket?
ALEX: Yeah.
CHARLIE: It's really nice, Alex.
ALEX: Thanks.
CHARLIE: Is it real leather?
ALEX: No, it isn't. It's synthetic.
CHARLIE: Are you sure?
ALEX: Yes. I'm sure.
CHARLIE: Well, see you.
ALEX: See you.

## Inner Voices

What are Alex and Charlie thinking during the conversation? Write their thoughts.

## CLOTHING FADS

Are clothes important to you? Are clothes important to students in your school? What are some popular types of clothing? What **brands** of clothing from different companies are popular? Are they expensive?

| TYPE OF CLOTHING | BRAND | PRICE |
|---|---|---|
| | | |
| | | |
| | | |
| | | |
| | | |
| | | |

**ASSERTING ONESELF/ROLE PLAY**

## ✔ COMMUNICATION TIP

**Getting your way politely**

A. Can I get through?
B. What?
A. I'd like to get by, please.
B. Oh. Sure.
A. Thanks.

Practice with a classmate. What are other situations like this in the halls? in the cafeteria? on the bus? Role-play some situations and present them to the class.

# School Dress Codes

In many schools there are rules about clothes. Some clothes are allowed. Other clothes aren't allowed. These rules are in a school's **dress code**.

Some clothes are very expensive. Some clothes are very sloppy. On other clothes there are words or pictures about drugs.

Some clothes are symbols of gangs. Beepers and cellular phones are expensive, noisy, and symbols of the drug trade. The clothes in these pictures aren't allowed in many schools.

## MADISON HIGH SCHOOL DRESS CODE

- ✗ No T-shirts with bad words or pictures
- ✗ No T-shirts with drug messages
- ✗ No hats or caps
- ✗ No bandanas
- ✗ No baggy jeans
- ✗ No net blouses
- ✗ No leggings or form-fitting pants
- ✗ No clothes with cut-outs
- ✗ No Walkmen
- ✗ No beepers
- ✗ No cellular phones

## YOUR SCHOOL DRESS CODE

Is there a dress code at your school? As a class, write your school's dress code. Discuss: Why is each type of clothing not allowed?

## Writing Clothes at My School

Write a paragraph about the kinds of clothes at your school.

OBSERVE AND RECORD — Go to the school library, cafeteria, or other busy place in your school. What different kinds of clothes do you see? Write your observations.

ORGANIZE YOUR IDEAS — Look at your observations. What are you going to write about first? second? third? Organize your ideas.

WRITE A FIRST DRAFT — Write a paragraph describing the different kinds of clothes at your school. Use this title: "Clothes at My School."

## THE WRITING PROCESS

- Pre-writing
- Organizing ideas
- Writing a first draft
- Revising
- Writing a final copy

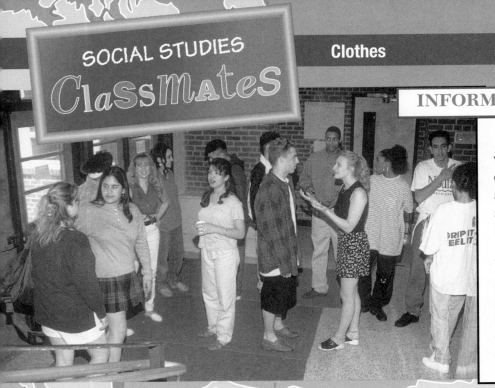

## INFORMATION IN PICTURES

These students are wearing many different kinds of clothes. Some students are wearing jeans. Some students are wearing shorts. Some girls are wearing skirts.

Some students are wearing long-sleeved shirts. Others are wearing short-sleeved shirts. Everyone is wearing shoes. Some students are wearing sneakers. Others are wearing sandals.

## PICTOGRAPHS

The photo above is one kind of picture. This graph is another kind of picture. It's called a **pictograph**. In this pictograph there is information about kinds of clothes and numbers of people.

The students in Room 207 are wearing different types of popular clothing. Seven students are wearing jeans today. Two students are wearing shorts. Three students are wearing skirts. With a classmate, ask and answer questions about the pictograph. (How many students are wearing . . . ?)

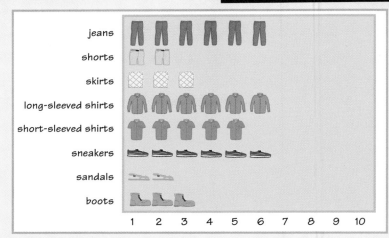

## MAKE A PICTOGRAPH!

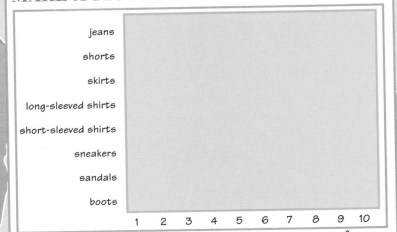

Look around your classroom. What are your classmates wearing today? Make a pictograph. What kinds of clothes are popular in your classroom?

## DESIGN A T-SHIRT!

Create a T-shirt for your class, your school, or your community. Share your T-shirt idea with the class. Describe your design. What is your T-shirt saying with pictures and words?

# CLOTHES AROUND THE WORLD

### INDIA

Prita is wearing a sari.

### SCOTLAND

John is wearing a kilt.

### JAPAN

Masako is wearing a kimono.

### THE PHILIPPINES

Susan is wearing a barong malong.

### AUSTRIA

Erika is wearing a dirndl.

### EGYPT

Anwar is wearing a galabiyah.

Where are these people from? What are they wearing? Describe their clothing. Is there clothing like this in your country? Describe it.

## INTERNATIONAL CLOTHING DAY!

Wear or bring to school some clothing from your culture. Describe the clothing for your classmates: What's the name of the clothing? Where is it from? Is the clothing popular today, or is it a traditional costume? Is it for special days or ceremonies? Is there a special meaning?

## PUBLISHING PROJECT!

As a class, create an international fashion magazine! Take photographs of students in their traditional clothing. Put each photo on a piece of paper with a paragraph about the photo. Bind the pages together to make a fashion magazine. Share it with other classes in your school.

## Research Project

Go to the library and find information about traditional costumes of different countries. Look in encyclopedias under *Clothing*. Also look for books on this subject. Choose a costume. Write about it and draw a picture. Make a presentation to the class.

## Saying and Solving Subtraction Problems

$$18 - 6 = 12 \qquad \begin{array}{r} 18 \\ -\ 6 \\ \hline 12 \end{array}$$

We say:
Eighteen minus six equals twelve.

---

**Say the math problems.**

1. $7 - 3 = 4$
2. $11 - 2 = 9$
3. $\begin{array}{r} 23 \\ -10 \\ \hline 13 \end{array}$
4. $38 - 16 = 22$
5. $\begin{array}{r} 34 \\ -\ 8 \\ \hline 26 \end{array}$

---

**Write the math problems two ways and say them.**

1. Nine minus five equals four.

   $9 - 5 = 4$

2. Seventeen minus six equals nine.

3. Eleven minus three equals eight.

4. Twenty-six minus one equals twenty-five.

5. Twenty-eight minus twelve equals sixteen.

6. Fourteen minus eleven equals three.

---

## WHAT DO YOU CALL THAT?

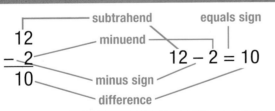

12 — minuend
− 2 — subtrahend
10 — difference

$12 - 2 = 10$ — minus sign, equals sign

A. What's the subtrahend?
B. *12.*
A. What's the minuend?
B. *2.*
A. What's the difference?
B. *10.*
A. How do you say the math problem?
B. *12 minus 2 equals 10.*

With a classmate, practice conversations about subtraction. Use the math problems in Exercises 1–6 above.

---

## Ways to Say It!

What's 11 minus 5?
11 minus 5 equals . . .
How much is 11 minus 5?
How much does 11 minus 5 equal?
How much is 11 take away 5?
Subtract 5 from 11.
Take 5 from 11.
What's the difference between 11 and 5?

Practice these different ways to say subtraction problems. Then work with a classmate. Ask each other easy subtraction problems and answer them. Try to use all the different ways to say the problems.

## Listening

Write and solve the subtraction problems you hear.

1. $7 - 2 = 5$
2. _____
3. _____
4. _____
5. _____
6. _____

The food service makes 50 pizzas every Friday. During the first lunch period, the students usually eat 30 pizzas. How many pizzas are usually left for the second lunch period?

A. What's the operation?
B. Subtraction.
A. What's the subtrahend?
B. *50.*
A. What's the minuend?
B. *30.*
A. What's the difference?
B. *20.*
A. So what's the answer to the problem?
B. *There are usually 20 pizzas left for the second lunch period.*

$$\begin{array}{r} 50 \\ -\ 30 \\ \hline 20 \end{array}$$

Solve these word problems. Then practice conversations about these problems with a classmate.

1. There are 100 windows in Northside High School. Thirty are cracked because of an earthquake last week. How many windows aren't broken?

$$\begin{array}{r} 100 \\ -\ 30 \\ \hline 70 \end{array}$$

2. There are 221 students at Stanton High School. There are 250 lockers. There's a locker for each student. How many extra lockers are there?

3. There are 84 classrooms in Lakewood High School. There are two floors in the school. Thirty-six classrooms are on the first floor. How many classrooms are on the second floor?

4. There are 30 players on the school tennis team. Thirteen are female. How many tennis players are male?

5. In the computer lab there are 35 computers. Eighteen computers aren't connected to a printer. How many computers are connected to a printer?

6. There are 150 families in the apartment building on Ocean Drive in Fort Lauderdale. A hurricane is coming, so 145 families are evacuating the building. How many families are staying?

Now make up two original word problems with subtraction, give them to a classmate, and practice conversations.

## Ways to Say It!

*There are 32 books *left*.
32 books *are left*.
There are 32 books *remaining*.*

Practice different ways to say differences. Then practice different ways to give the answers to Exercises 1–6 above.

# ClassMates
## CAREER PROFILE

## Home Economics Teacher

Sarah W. Hrobowski
Home Economics Teacher

EDUCATION: Bachelor of Science (B.S.) in Vocational Home Economics

Master of Science (M.S.) degree in Administration

Coursework in Vocational Education

JOB DESCRIPTION: Teach cooking

Teach the business of catering

WORK LOCATION: High school home economics classroom

QUOTE: "We want to make a difference in the lives of our students. We give all of our students a job skill."

---

## SELF-ASSESSMENT CHECKLIST
## Check It Out!

I know:

- [ ] names of clothing
- [ ] brands of clothing
- [ ] my school dress code
- [ ] clothes around the world

I know how to:

- [ ] get my way politely
- [ ] read a school dress code
- [ ] write a paragraph about clothing in my school
- [ ] interpret a pictograph
- [ ] make a pictograph
- [ ] create and publish a magazine photo essay
- [ ] do research to make a presentation
- [ ] say, write, and solve subtraction problems
- [ ] solve and talk about word problems with subtraction

# Back to School Night

9

*I*n this chapter, we will cover the following topics and skills:

**SCHOOL COMMUNICATION**
➤ A principal's welcoming speech to parents
➤ Giving a speech

**SOCIAL STUDIES**
➤ Greetings around the world
➤ Cross-cultural interviews

**LANGUAGE ARTS**
➤ Subject and verb agreement

**MATH**
➤ Word problems with multiplication

**COMMUNICATION TIP**
➤ Introducing teachers and parents

**CAREER PROFILE**
➤ High school principal

**ASSESSMENT**
➤ Self-assessment checklist

What are the parents doing in these pictures?

Choose the correct words to complete the principal's speech.

Good evening, parents. My name is Muriel Santiago. I'm the principal here at Chestertown High School. I'm pleased to welcome you to Back to School Night. Let me introduce our wonderful faculty and staff here at Chestertown High. Mr. Peter Braniff and Mrs. Viviana Salgado are our Math teachers. They ( teach  teaches )**1** your children every day. Mr. Glen Gordon ( teach  teaches )**2** History. Your children ( study  studies )**3** English with Ms. Linda Webb and Mr. John Paxton. Our P.E. teachers, Mr. Alan Perez and Miss Jenny Liu, ( play  plays )**4** sports and ( do  does )**5** exercises with our children in our beautiful new gym. Our school chorus ( sing  sings )**6** and our band ( practice  practices )**7** with our talented music teacher, Mrs. Marie Kamana. All of you know Mrs. Clark, our school secretary. She ( work  works )**8** in the office and ( answer  answers )**9** all your questions. Our school nurse, Mrs. Capelli, ( take  takes )**10** good care of your children every day. Our custodians, Mr. Ronald Henry and Ms. Clara Long, ( clean  cleans )**11** our school and ( make  makes )**12** our school a happy place. Our guidance counselor, Ms. Taylor, ( help  helps )**13** your children with their problems and their college applications. Our librarian, Mrs. Mary Herrington, and her assistant, Mr. Joseph Allen, ( help  helps )**14** your children with their research projects. And finally, I'm happy to introduce Officer Silvia Martinez, our security officer from the Police Department. She ( speak  speaks )**15** four languages, ( understand  understands )**16** our students' problems, and ( teach  teaches )**17** our classes on safety and drug abuse. Please give our faculty and staff a big round of applause.

**Now give the speech. Read it to your classmates.**

## Act It Out!

It's Back to School Night at your school. You're the principal! Welcome the parents and introduce the faculty and staff.

Hello. My name is Karen Martin. I'm your children's English language teacher. Your children study with me for two periods every day. Every day in class your children are very busy.

A. I'm sorry I'm late. I'm Wendy Long's mother.
B. Hello. My name is Karen Martin. I'm Wendy's English language teacher. Your child studies with me for two periods every day. Every day in class your child is very busy.

| | |
|---|---|
| They study grammar. | She ___studies___ grammar. |
| They talk about the news. | She _____ about the news. |
| They write in their journals. | She _____ in her journal. |
| They read literature. | She _____ literature. |
| They work in pairs and groups. | She _____ in pairs and groups. |
| They use the computer. | She _____ the computer. |
| They practice pronunciation. | She _____ pronunciation. |
| They go to the library and do research. | She _____ to the library and _____ research. |
| Every Friday they take a test. | Every Friday she _____ a test. |
| Your children work very hard, and they do very well in my class. | Your child _____ very hard, and she _____ very well in my class. |

 **COMMUNICATION TIP**

**Introducing teachers and parents**

ISABEL: Mr. Price, I'd like to introduce my parents, Mr. and Mrs. Vargas. Mom and Dad, this is Mr. Price. He's my Science teacher.

MR. PRICE: It's nice to meet you, Mr. and Mrs. Vargas.

MRS. VARGAS: Nice to meet you.

MR. VARGAS: Hello.

In a small group, practice conversations that introduce teachers and parents to each other. Use your own names and the names of your teachers.

● Some people shake hands.

● Some people kiss.

● Some people hug.

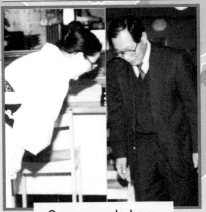

● Some people bow.

Greetings are different in different parts of the world. In North America, most men greet each other with a handshake. Some women shake hands, too. In France, friends and neighbors kiss on both cheeks. People bow in many Asian countries. Of course, sometimes people just smile and say "Hello."

● Some people look at the other person and smile.

Discuss greetings with your classmates.

How do you greet people in your culture?

How do you greet your classmates?
How do you greet members of your family?
What are the differences?

How do you greet adults? How do you greet children? What are the differences?

Do you greet men and women the same way? How do you greet strangers?

## CROSS-CULTURAL INTERVIEW

Interview people from two or more different countries. Ask them about greetings in their countries. How do people greet each other in families? in school? at work? How do people greet adults? children? men? women? strangers? Report your information to the class.

# Language Arts ClassMates

## Subject & Verb Agreement

In every sentence there are a *subject* and a *verb*. The subject is a person or a thing. The verb is an action. The subject is *singular* or *plural*. The verb agrees with the subject.

Karla practices English.
↑ ↑
Singular    Verb
Subject

The students practice English.
↑ ↑
Plural    Verb
Subject

The parents talk talks to the teacher on Back to School Night.

A. What's the subject?
B. *The parents*.
A. Is the subject singular or plural?
B. *Plural*.
A. Which verb agrees with the subject—*talk* or *talks*?
B. *Talk*.

Choose the word to complete each sentence. Then practice conversations about the sentences with a classmate.

1. Mr. Robinson ( teach (teaches) ) Computer Science.
2. In our class, the students ( speak   speaks ) many different languages.
3. Miss Ruiz ( give   gives ) tests every Friday.
4. I ( play   plays ) on the baseball team.
5. Jenny and Rosa ( do   does ) well in English class.
6. Every afternoon they ( study   studies ) for three hours in the library.
7. Thuy, Lily, and Selma ( sing   sings ) in the school chorus.
8. We ( know   knows ) the principal very well.
9. Mr. Rooney ( help   helps ) students every Wednesday after school.
10. Every Monday the class ( go   goes ) to the computer lab.
11. All Math students ( take   takes ) a test every Tuesday.
12. From 10:00 to 10:30, Ms. Lane's students ( write   writes ) in their journals.

## Saying and Solving Multiplication Problems

$$\begin{array}{r} 3 \\ \times\ 4 \\ \hline 12 \end{array}$$

$3 \times 4 = 12$

We say: Three times four equals twelve.

---

Say the math problems.

**1** $2 \times 4 = 8$

**2** $6 \times 3 = 18$

**3** $\begin{array}{r} 7 \\ \times\ 5 \\ \hline 35 \end{array}$

**4** $11 \times 8 = 88$

**5** $\begin{array}{r} 12 \\ \times\ 7 \\ \hline 84 \end{array}$

---

Write the math problems two ways and say them.

**1** Five times four equals twenty.

$5 \times 4 = 20$ $\quad\quad \begin{array}{r} 5 \\ \times\ 4 \\ \hline 20 \end{array}$

**2** Nine times three equals twenty-seven.

.

**3** Four times eleven equals forty-four.

**4** Six times seven equals forty-two.

**5** Ten times six equals sixty.

**6** Twelve times three equals thirty-six.

---

# WHAT DO YOU CALL THAT ?

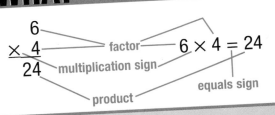

$$\begin{array}{r} 6 \\ \times\ 4 \\ \hline 24 \end{array}$$

factor — $6 \times 4 = 24$

multiplication sign

equals sign

product

A. What are the factors?
B. *6 and 4.*
A. What's the product?
B. *24.*
A. How do you say the math problem?
B. *6 times 4 equals 24.*

With a classmate, practice conversations about multiplication. Use the math problems in Exercises 1–6 above.

---

## Ways to Say It!

What's 5 times 3?
Multiply 5 times 3.
5 times 3 equals . . .
How much is 5 times 3?
What's the product of 5 times 3?
Find the product of 5 and 3.

Practice these different ways to say multiplication problems. Then work with a classmate. Ask each other easy multiplication problems and answer them. Try to use all the different ways to say the problems.

---

## Listening

Write and solve the multiplication problems you hear.

**1** $\underline{9 \times 4 = 36}$
**2** _____
**3** _____
**4** _____
**5** _____
**5** _____

## Word Problems with Multiplication

$$\begin{array}{r} 4 \\ \times\ 3 \\ \hline 12 \end{array}$$

There are 4 grades at Gresham High School. Three children from each grade play the violin in the school orchestra. How many students play the violin in the orchestra?

A. What's the operation?
B. Multiplication.
A. What are the factors?
B. *3* and *4*.
A. What's the product?
B. *12.*
A. So what's the answer to the problem?
B. *12 students play the violin.*

Solve these word problems. Then practice conversations about these problems with a classmate.

1. Ms. Farida teaches 6 periods of Math. There are 20 students in each class. How many students does Ms. Farida teach?

$$\begin{array}{r} 20 \\ \times\ 6 \\ \hline 120 \end{array}$$

2. Every Wednesday, the food service makes 3 different kinds of pizzas for lunch. The food service makes 40 pizzas of each kind. How many pizzas do they make?

3. In Mr. Paul's English class there are 28 students. There are a dictionary, a textbook, and a workbook for each student on Mr. Paul's bookshelf. How many books are on Mr. Paul's bookshelf?

4. There are 5 boxes of new books for the library. There are 20 books in each box. How many books are there for the library?

5. On the school tennis team, there are 12 students from each of the four grades. How many students are on the tennis team?

6. The school is using 5 buses on a field trip. There are 35 students on each bus. How many students are going on the field trip?

7. There are 150 books on each bookshelf in the school library. There are 50 bookshelves. How many books are there in the school library?

8. Every day the bell rings before and after each class period. There are 8 class periods. How many times does the bell ring every day?

Now make up two original word problems with multiplication, give them to a classmate, and practice conversations.

## High School Principal

Donald L. Clausen
High School Principal

| | |
|---|---|
| EDUCATION: | Bachelor of Science (B.S.) degree in Health and Physical Education |
| | Master of Education (M.Ed.) degree |
| JOB DESCRIPTION: | Responsible for all high school programs, 2,000 students, and a staff of 200 people |
| WORK LOCATION: | Main office of a high school |
| QUOTE: | "I work with many kinds of people. Every day is different and full of different challenges." |

## ✓ Check It Out!

**I know:**
- ☐ school personnel and their functions
- ☐ classroom activities
- ☐ greetings around the world

**I know how to:**
- ☐ give a welcoming speech
- ☐ introduce teachers and parents
- ☐ interview people about cultural differences
- ☐ identify subjects and verbs in sentence
- ☐ describe subject and verb agreement
- ☐ say, write, and solve multiplication problems
- ☐ solve and talk about word problems with multiplication

# Extracurricular Activities

**10**

*In* this chapter, we will cover the following topics and skills:

**SCHOOL COMMUNICATION**
➤ Extracurricular activities
➤ Interviewing a schoolmate
➤ Extracurricular activity questionnaire
➤ Extracurricular activities in your school

**MATH**
➤ Word problems with division

**READING AND WRITING**
➤ Reading a schedule
➤ The Writing Process: *Pre-writing, Organizing ideas, Writing a first draft, Revising, Publishing*
➤ Writing a newspaper article

**COMMUNICATION TIP**
➤ Asking a question

**CAREER PROFILE**
➤ School athletic director

**ASSESSMENT**
➤ Self-assessment checklist

**What are the students doing?**

**MONDAY**
6:00 AM Swim
3:30 PM Basketball practice

**TUESDAY**
6:00 AM Swim
3:30 PM Soccer practice

**WEDNESDAY**
6:00 AM Swim
3:15 PM Tutor

**THURSDAY**
6:00 AM Swim
4:15 PM Choir practice

**FRIDAY**
6:00 AM Swim
5:00 PM Volunteer—Homeless Shelter

**SATURDAY**
Help at the grocery store

**SUNDAY**
Help at the grocery store

BARBARA: So, Tomás, you're our school's "Outstanding Citizen of the Year." How does it feel?

TOMÁS: It feels great!

BARBARA: You're a very busy person. Tell me about your daily schedule.

TOMÁS: Well, Barbara, I get up early every day, eat a good breakfast, and run to the pool.

BARBARA: What time do you get to the pool?

TOMÁS: I get there at 6:00 every morning, and I swim with the swim team for an hour. Then I take a shower, get dressed, and run to my first period class.

BARBARA: And what do you do after school?

TOMÁS: On Monday, I play basketball. On Tuesday, I play soccer. On Wednesday, I tutor children at an elementary school. On Thursday, I sing in the choir. On Friday, I volunteer at the homeless shelter.

BARBARA: What do you do there?

TOMÁS: Sometimes I serve meals, and sometimes I do yardwork.

BARBARA: And what do you do on weekends?

TOMÁS: Well, I help my parents at the family's grocery store on weekends.

BARBARA: Wow! You're so busy! How are your grades?

TOMÁS: I get good grades.

BARBARA: Tomás, how do you do it?

TOMÁS: Do what?

BARBARA: How do you have time for everything?

TOMÁS: I'm organized, I guess, and I work hard.

BARBARA: Well, congratulations!

TOMÁS: Thanks.

# CENTRAL HIGH SCHOOL TIMES

Vol. 47 No. 8                                                                  May

## Tomás Rueda Is Outstanding Citizen of the Year!

by Barbara Seton

Tomás Rueda is the outstanding citizen of the year. He's a very busy person!

Every morning, Tomás ___gets___<sup>1</sup> up at 6 o'clock. He _____<sup>2</sup> a good breakfast and _____<sup>3</sup> to the pool. He _____<sup>4</sup> for an hour, _____<sup>5</sup> a shower, _____<sup>6</sup> dressed, and _____<sup>7</sup> to his first period class.

He's busy every afternoon. On Monday, he _____<sup>8</sup> basketball. On Tuesday, he _____<sup>9</sup> soccer. On Wednesday, he _____<sup>10</sup> children at the elementary school. On Thursday, he _____<sup>11</sup> in the choir. On Friday, he _____<sup>12</sup> at the homeless shelter. Sometimes he _____<sup>13</sup> meals, and sometimes he _____<sup>14</sup> yardwork.

Every weekend Tomás _____<sup>15</sup> his parents at the family's grocery store.

Tomás Rueda tutors children at an elementary school.

Tomás Rueda is very busy all the time, and he _____<sup>16</sup> good grades. Everybody at Central High School congratulates Tomás Rueda — outstanding citizen of the year.

Fill in the missing words to complete the school newspaper article.

**✔ COMMUNICATION TIP**

**Asking a Question**

A. Excuse me, *Mrs. Henderson.* Can I ask you a question?
B. Sure. What is it?
A. *When does the spring vacation start?*
B. *Next Thursday.*

Practice with some classmates. Ask some questions.

# *Writing* A Newspaper Article

Write an article about a schoolmate.

**THE WRITING PROCESS**

- *Pre-writing*
- *Organizing ideas*
- *Writing a first draft*
- *Revising*
- *Writing a final copy*

INTERVIEW    Interview a student in your school. (Don't interview a classmate. Interview somebody you don't know. Your teacher can help you.) In your interview, ask about the student's daily activities. Take notes during the interview.

ORGANIZE YOUR IDEAS    Look at your notes. What are you going to write about first? second? third? Organize your ideas.

WRITE A FIRST DRAFT    Write a newspaper article about the student. Give your article a headline.

REVISE    Show your article to your teacher. Revise your article.

PUBLISH    Put all the articles from your class together and make copies. Give copies to the student you interview, your classmates, and other students in your school. As a class, choose one article and give it to your school newspaper to publish.

## *Classmates Exchange* Autograph Hunt

A. Do you play basketball?
B. No, I don't.

A. Do you play basketball?
B. Yes, I do.
A. Where do you play basketball?
B. At the YMCA.
A. Sign here, please.

A. Do you belong to a club?
B. No, I don't.

A. Do you belong to a club?
B. Yes, I do.
A. What club do you belong to?
B. The International Club.
A. Sign here, please.

Circulate around the room and ask classmates questions about extracurricular activities. Collect classmates' signatures and ask for more information. Put the signatures and information on the form on page 81.

80

# Extracurricular Activity Questionnaire

| WHO . . . | SIGNATURE | MORE INFORMATION |
|---|---|---|
| plays basketball? | _____ | _____ |
| plays football? | _____ | _____ |
| plays soccer? | _____ | _____ |
| plays tennis? | _____ | _____ |
| plays chess? | _____ | _____ |
| plays ping-pong? | _____ | _____ |
| plays badminton? | _____ | _____ |
| sings in the choir? | _____ | _____ |
| volunteers? | _____ | _____ |
| tutors? | _____ | _____ |
| babysits? | _____ | _____ |
| works? | _____ | _____ |
| belongs to a club? | _____ | _____ |

## GET INVOLVED!

Are you involved in extracurricular activities in your school? It's a great way to learn new things, to practice English, and to make new friends. As a class, make a list of extracurricular activities in your school. Who organizes the activity? Write the sponsor's name. Where and when does the activity meet? Write the location, day, and time.

| ACTIVITY | SPONSOR | LOCATION | DAY/TIME |
|---|---|---|---|
| _____ | _____ | _____ | _____ |
| _____ | _____ | _____ | _____ |
| _____ | _____ | _____ | _____ |
| _____ | _____ | _____ | _____ |
| _____ | _____ | _____ | _____ |
| _____ | _____ | _____ | _____ |
| _____ | _____ | _____ | _____ |
| _____ | _____ | _____ | _____ |

It's your school and these are your extracurricular activities. Which activity interests you? Talk to the sponsor and sign up. Get involved!

## DESIGN A POSTER!

Create a poster to advertise an extracurricular activity in your school. Use pictures and words to tell about the activity. Make your poster exciting!

# Saying and Solving Division Problems

$$3\overline{)24}^{\,8} \qquad 24 \div 3 = 8$$

Twenty-four divided by three equals eight.

**Say the math problems.**

① $8\overline{)16}^{\,2}$  ② $40 \div 4 = 10$  ③ $72 \div 8 = 9$  ④ $27 \div 3 = 9$  ⑤ $9\overline{)54}^{\,6}$

**Write the math problems two ways and say them.**

① Ten divided by two equals five.

$$10 \div 2 = 5 \qquad 2\overline{)10}^{\,5}$$

② Thirty-six divided by four equals nine.

③ Twenty divided by five equals four.

④ Forty-eight divided by eight equals six.

⑤ Fifty-six divided by seven equals eight.

⑥ Fifty divided by five equals ten.

## WHAT DO YOU CALL THAT ?

quotient

$$6\overline{)42}^{\,7}$$

dividend

divisor

$42 \div 6 = 7$

equals sign

A. What's the dividend?
B. 42.
A. What's the divisor?
B. 6.
A. What's the quotient?
B. 7.
A. How do you say the math problem?
B. *42 divided by 6 equals 7.*

With a classmate, practice conversations about division. Use the math problems in Exercises 1–6 above.

## Ways to Say It

What's 15 divided by 3?
15 divided by 3 equals . . .
How much is 15 divided by 3?
How much does 15 divided by 3 equal?
Divide 15 by 3.
Divide 3 into 15.

Practice these different ways to say division problems. Then work with a classmate. Ask each other easy division problems and answer them. Try to use all the different ways to say the problems.

## Listening

Write the division problems you hear.

① $36 \div 9 = 4$
② _____
③ _____
④ _____
⑤ _____
⑥ _____

# Word Problems with Division

18 cheerleaders are practicing on the football field. The cheerleaders are practicing in groups of 3. How many groups of cheerleaders are there?

A. What's the operation?
B. Division.
A. What's the dividend?
B. *18.*
A. What's the divisor?
B. *3.*
A. What's the quotient?
B. *6.*
A. So what's the answer to the problem?
B. *There are 6 groups of cheerleaders.*

$$3\overline{)18} = 6$$

Solve these word problems. Then practice conversations about these problems with a classmate.

1. There are 27 students in Mrs. Dixon's math class. The students work in groups of 3. How many groups are there?

   $27 \div 3 = 9$

2. There are 120 students in Mr. Sear's P.E. class. The students stand in 8 equal rows for their exercises. How many students are in each row?

3. There are 210 students in Westwood High School. There are 3 lunch periods with equal numbers of students. How many students eat at each lunch period?

4. There are 50 students in the computer lab during third period. There are 25 computers. How many students work together on each computer?

5. There are 24 students on the school tennis team. The team practices in groups of 4. How many groups are there?

6. There are 45 students in the International Club. Equal numbers of students are from 5 different countries. How many students are from each country?

7. There are 12 students in the Drama Club. Equal numbers of students are from the 10th, 11th, and 12th grades. How many 10th graders are in the Drama Club?

8. There are 28 students in the Science lab. The students work in pairs. How many pairs of students work together?

Now make up two original word problems with division, give them to a classmate, and practice conversations.

## School Athletic Director

Angelo Hilios
School Athletic Director

EDUCATION: Bachelor of Science (B.S.) degree in Social Studies

Master of Arts (M.A.) degree in Administration and Supervision

JOB DESCRIPTION: Responsible for all athletic events and all other activities at the school building

WORK LOCATION: High school

QUOTE: "I enjoy young adults, and I like sports and games."

---

**SELF-ASSESSMENT CHECKLIST**

## Check It Out!

**I know:**
- [ ] extracurricular activities
- [ ] opportunities for extracurricular activities in my school
- [ ] sponsors, locations, and meeting times of extracurricular activities in my school

**I know how to:**
- [ ] read a schedule
- [ ] ask a question
- [ ] interview a schoolmate
- [ ] write a newspaper article using the writing process
- [ ] ask classmates about their activities
- [ ] say, write, and solve division problems
- [ ] solve and talk about word problems with division

# Dating and Relationships

**11**

*I*n this chapter, we will cover the following topics and skills:

**SCHOOL COMMUNICATION**
➤ Dating customs
➤ Dating customs in other cultures

**MATH**
➤ Word problems with mixed operations

**READING AND WRITING**
➤ Journal entry: A friend
➤ The Writing Process: Pre-writing, Organizing ideas, Writing a first draft

**SOCIAL STUDIES**
➤ Marriage around the world

**COMMUNICATION TIP**
➤ Making, accepting, and rejecting invitations

**CAREER PROFILE**
➤ School psychologist

**ASSESSMENT**
➤ Self-assessment checklist

Who are these people? How do you think they feel about each other?

# Do You Go Out on Dates?

SALLY: How often do you and your boyfriend see each other?

BECCA: Not very often. We aren't in the same classes, so I rarely see him at school. Sometimes I bump into him in the hallway.

SALLY: Do you talk on the telephone?

BECCA: Yeah. Sometimes I call him. Sometimes he calls me.

SALLY: Do you go out on dates?

BECCA: Rarely. He has a part-time job at a restaurant on weekends, and I often have babysitting jobs on Friday and Saturday evenings. Sometimes we go to the movies.

SALLY: Do you ever go out to eat at a restaurant?

BECCA: Never! We don't have money to go to restaurants.

## Classmates Exchange

Have a conversation with a classmate. Talk about how often you and a good friend see each other. When do you get together? Where? What do you do?

## Classmates Journal

Write about a friend. Who is it? Why is this person your friend? Write your ideas in your journal.

## CROSS-CULTURAL EXPLORATIONS

### Dating Customs

In pairs, in small groups, or as a class, compare dating customs in two different cultures.

Do young people go out on dates?

How old are they when they begin to date?

Do they usually go as a pair or as a group?

Who usually pays?

Does somebody (a chaperone) go with them?

Where do young people go on a date?

Do parents usually know their children's friends?

**Making, accepting, and rejecting invitations**

A. Would you like to *go to the dance Friday night?*

B. Sure. I'd love to.

A. Would you like to *go to the movies Saturday night?*

B. No, I don't think so.

Practice invitations with your classmates.

## *Ways to Say It!*

### Rejecting Invitations and Advances

No, thank you.
I'm just not interested.
I'm busy.
I don't date.

I don't go out on dates.
My parents don't allow me to date.
I'm not allowed.

## THE WRITING PROCESS

- **Pre-writing**
- **Organizing ideas**
- **Writing a first draft**
- Revising
- Writing a final copy

**USING A GRAPHIC ORGANIZER**

## *Writing* My Friend and I

Write a paragraph about you and a friend.

BRAINSTORM   Think about a good friend. Do you and your friend have the same interests or different interests? Do you both enjoy the same sports? activities? food? clothes? movies? music? classes? **Brainstorm** your ideas and write them in the Venn diagram. This Venn diagram has three sections: one to list your friend's interests, one to list your interests, and one to list the interests you both have.

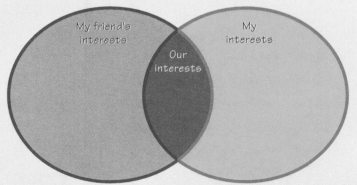

My friend's interests

My interests

Our interests

ORGANIZE YOUR IDEAS   Look at the Venn diagram. What are you going to write about first? second? third? Organize your ideas.

WRITE A FIRST DRAFT   Write a first draft about you and your friend.

# ClassMates

## Marriage Around the World

A wedding is an important event. It's a special day for the bride and the groom. They're getting married. They're beginning a new life together. It's also a special day for their families and friends. They come together to celebrate with the bride and the groom. People all over the world have weddings, and weddings are different in different places.

Where do you think these weddings are happening? How are they different?

### Some North American Wedding Customs

The bride holds flowers during the wedding ceremony. After the ceremony, she throws the flowers to the single women at the wedding. According to custom, the woman who catches the flowers will be the next to get married.

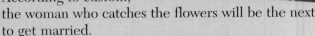

People throw rice at the bride and groom after the wedding. According to custom, the rice brings good luck and many children.

The bride and groom give each other wedding rings. The ring is a circle. A circle has no end. This means the marriage will not end.

## What Do You Think?

How do you celebrate weddings in your culture? Think about the following questions:

When do people have weddings?
Where do they have weddings?
How long are wedding celebrations?
What do the bride and groom wear?
What do the guests wear?
Who performs the ceremony?
What do the bride and groom say during the wedding ceremony?
Who else speaks during the wedding ceremony?
Is there music?
Is there a celebration after the ceremony?
What do people eat at the celebration?
What gifts do people give the bride and groom?

## What's Your Opinion?

In some cultures, parents arrange the marriages of their children. They choose their son's bride or their daughter's groom. What do you think about this custom?

What's a good age for people to get married? Give reasons for your answer.

Make a poster that shows wedding customs in your culture. Report to the class about these customs. Use your poster in your presentation.

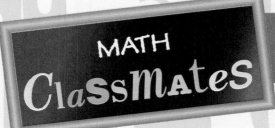

## Word Problems with Mixed Operations

In the cafeteria, there are 80 tables for students and 10 tables for faculty and staff. How many tables are there in all?

A. What's the operation?
B. *Addition.*
A. What are the *addends?*
B. *80 and 10.*
A. What's the *sum?*
B. *90.*
A. So what's the answer to the problem?
B. *There are 90 tables in the cafeteria.*

There are 60 students in the school orchestra. The school orchestra takes school buses to concerts at other schools. Each bus holds 30 students. How many buses does the orchestra need?

A. What's the operation?
B. *Division.*
A. What's the *dividend?*
B. *60.*
A. What's the *divisor?*
B. *30.*
A. What's the *quotient?*
B. *2.*
A. So what's the answer to the problem?
B. *The orchestra needs 2 buses.*

Solve these word problems. Then practice conversations about these problems with a classmate.

1. There are 50 tables in the school cafeteria. During the first lunch period, 8 students sit at each table. How many students eat during the first lunch period?

$$\begin{array}{r} 50 \\ \times\ 8 \\ \hline 400 \end{array}$$

2. There are 200 students at the school dance. 120 male students are at the dance. How many female students are there?

3. There are 2000 students at Eastern High School. Five guidance counselors help equal numbers of students. How many students does each guidance counselor help?

4. There are 50 lockers on each floor of Wilson High School. There are 3 floors in the school. How many lockers are there in the school?

5. The school tennis team practices in pairs. There are 38 students on the team. How many pairs practice?

6. 28 female students and 43 male students are on the track team. How many students are on the school track team?

7. On Back to School Night, there are 36 teachers and office staff on the stage. Four are office staff. How many teachers are on stage?

8. There are 52 students in the computer lab. The students work in pairs. How many pairs of students work together?

Now make up four original word problems, one for each operation—addition, subtraction, multiplication, and division. Give the problems to a classmate and practice conversations.

## School Psychologist

| | |
|---|---|
| EDUCATION: | Bachelor of Arts (B.A.) degree in Psychology |
| | Master of Arts (M.A.) degree in Psychology |
| JOB DESCRIPTION: | Evaluate academic, social, and emotional needs of students |
| | Consult with parents and teachers |
| | Teach coping skills and problem-solving skills through counseling |
| WORK LOCATION: | Guidance office of a high school |
| QUOTE: | "I like to help students of all ages." |

Terry Aliabadi
School Psychologist

### SELF-ASSESSMENT CHECKLIST

## Check It Out!

**I know:**
- [ ] dating customs
- [ ] different ways to reject invitations and advances
- [ ] wedding customs around the world

**I know how to:**
- [ ] compare dating customs in different cultures
- [ ] make, accept, and reject invitations
- [ ] brainstorm ideas for writing
- [ ] use a Venn diagram
- [ ] write about my interests
- [ ] solve and talk about word problems with mixed operations

# Emotions

*In this chapter, we will cover the following topics and skills:*

**SCHOOL COMMUNICATION**
➤ Feelings and emotions
➤ Classroom survey
➤ Graphing information

**MATH**
➤ Place value

**SOCIAL STUDIES**
➤ Patchwork quilts

**COMMUNICATION TIP**
➤ Greeting friends

**LITERATURE**
➤ I'm in a Rotten Mood by Jack Prelutsky

**CAREER PROFILE**
➤ Teen Health Educator

**ASSESSMENT**
➤ Self-assessment checklist

**How do these students feel? How do you know?**

# You're Biting Your Nails!

| | |
|---|---|
| LILA: | Renzo, you look nervous! |
| RENZO: | Me? Nervous? Why do you say that? |
| LILA: | You're biting your nails. |
| RENZO: | I am? |
| LILA: | Yes. You don't usually bite your nails. |
| RENZO: | You're right. I don't. |
| LILA: | Why are you nervous? |
| RENZO: | I guess it's because I have a big science test tomorrow. |
| LILA: | Oh, I see. Well, good luck on the test. |
| RENZO: | Thanks. |

## Classmates Exchange

A. What makes you *nervous?*
B. *Tests.*
A. What do you do when you're *nervous?*
B. When I'm *nervous, I sweat a lot.*

**Practice the conversation with a classmate.**

**Then create new conversations with other words that describe how people feel:** *sad, angry, happy, embarrassed, tired.*

## COMMUNICATION TIP

**Greeting friends**

A. Hi, *Ramon*. How are you?
B. *Fine*. How about you?
A. *I'm great*.

Practice greetings with your classmates.

## Ways to Say It!

| Greeting People | Responding to Greetings | |
|---|---|---|
| How are you? | Fine. | I'm fine. |
| How are you doing? | Okay. | I'm okay. |
| How's it going? | All right. | I'm all right. |
| How are things? | Great. | I'm great. |
| | Good. | I'm good. |

# ClassMates LITERATURE

## I'm in a Rotten Mood!

by Jack Prelutsky

I'm in a rotten mood today,
a really rotten mood today,
I'm feeling cross,
I'm feeling mean,
I'm jumpy as a jumping bean,
I have an awful attitude—
I'M IN A ROTTEN MOOD!

I'm in a rotten mood today,
a really rotten mood today,
I'm in a snit, I'm in a stew,
there's nothing that I care to do
but sit all by myself and brood—
I'M IN A ROTTEN MOOD!

I'm in a rotten mood today,
a really rotten mood today,
you'd better stay away from me,
I'm just a lump of misery,
I'm feeling absolutely rude—
I'M IN A ROTTEN MOOD!

from Jack Prelutksy, *The New
Kid on the Block*. New York:
Greenwillow Books, 1984.

### THE WRITER'S CRAFT

**Repetition**
Writers use repetition when they repeat sounds as words or sentences. The repetition of sounds gives the poem a musical feeling. The poet Jack Prelutsky repeats the sentence *I'm in a rotten mood today* at the beginning and at the end of every stanza. What other examples of repetition are there in "I'm in a Rotten Mood"?

### Create a Poem!

Write a poem about an emotion.
Try to use repetition in your poem.

# ClassMates

## Patchwork Quilts

This woman is making a patchwork quilt. Quilts are an example of folk art. Many people put quilts on their beds or hang them on their walls as pictures.

Some quilts tell stories about people or events. Some quilts tell about the history of a family, a town, or a culture. Some quilts show the quilter's emotions. Other quilts don't have a story or message. They are just beautiful designs.

First the quilter draws a picture on paper. Then the quilter cuts out pieces of cloth and sews them together. Some quilters use a sewing machine. Other quilters sew quilts by hand.

Faith Ringgold, *Sonny's Quilt.* 84½" × 60". Acrylic on canvas, pieced borders. Collection of Barbara and Ronald Davis Balsar.

*Sonny's Quilt*, Faith Ringgold

The American quilter Faith Ringgold made this quilt in 1986. What do you see in *Sonny's Quilt*? The person in this quilt is Faith Ringgold's friend Sonny Rollins. What does the quilter tell you about Sonny?

*Sunshine and Shadow*, Susan Beechy

Does this quilt tell a story or show feelings? What do you think of when you look at this quilt?

Susan Beechy (Topeka, Indiana), *Sunshine and Shadow*, 1935–1940. Machine-pieced, hand-quilted cotton, 88¼" × 73¾". Collection of the Museum of American Folk Art, New York. Gift of David Pottinger.

## Design a Quilt!

Design a quilt that tells a story or shows how you feel. Draw a design on graph paper and color it.

## Classmates Folk Art Museum

Folk art is the art of everyday life. Folk art can be household objects, furniture, toys, clothes, pictures, signs, or anything.

Do you have an example of folk art from your culture? Bring it to class. Tell your classmates about it. Who designed it? What is it made of? What is it used for? Does it tell a story?

**FINE ARTS CONNECTION**

**Weather vane, unknown, 1850-1875**

Make a classroom museum display of the folk art. Write museum labels to describe each item: the name of the object, the name of the artist, the name of the culture or country, the materials, and other information about the object. On the label, also write the name of the donor — the student who brings in the object. Invite other classes to visit your museum. Stand next to your object and answer questions about it.

# MATH ClassMates

**3,879**

| thousands | hundreds | tens | ones |
|-----------|----------|------|------|
| 3 | 8 | 7 | 9 |

| Value | 3,000 | 800 | 70 | 9 |
|-------|-------|-----|-----|---|

3,879 is a four-digit number. It has four digits: 3, 8, 7, and 9. Each digit has a different value. The value of the digit depends on its place in the number. This is called the **place value**.

- The 3 is in the thousands place. Its value is 3,000.
- The 8 is in the hundreds place. Its value is 800.
- The 7 is in the tens place. Its value is 70.
- The 9 is in the ones place. Its value is 9.

The standard form for writing this number is:   3,879
The expanded form is:   3,000 + 800 + 70 + 9.

$$
\begin{array}{r}
3,000 \\
800 \\
70 \\
+\quad 9 \\
\hline
3,879
\end{array}
$$

**three thousands**
3 × 1,000 = 3,000

**eight hundreds**
8 × 100 = 800

**3,879**

**seven tens**
7 × 10 = 70

**nine ones**
9 × 1 = 9

**With a classmate, give each other numbers and ask about the digits.**

A.  Where's the *8*?
B.  *The eight is in the hundreds place.*
A.  What's its value?
B.  Its value is *800*.

## Classmates Exchange

With a classmate, say each number. Then decide the value of each underlined digit.

1. 1<u>2</u>1
2. 3,06<u>2</u>
3. 5,<u>9</u>02
4. <u>4</u>,890
5. <u>2</u>,476
6. 7,<u>9</u>61
7. 1,<u>4</u>34
8. 6,2<u>0</u>7

## Listening

Listen and circle the correct number.

1. (14)      40
2. 16      60
3. 590      950
4. 217      271
5. 691      961
6. 7,945      9,755
7. 8,531      8,913
8. 3,043      3,304

## Teen Health Educator

Kelly S. McKittrick
Teen Health Educator

| | |
|---|---|
| **EDUCATION:** | Bachelor of Science (B.S.) degree in General Studies |
| | Master of Arts (M.A.) degree in Health Education |
| **JOB DESCRIPTION:** | Teach teens how to take care of themselves |
| | Supervise a telephone hotline for teenagers |
| | (Through the hotline, teens have a place to get help from someone their own age.) |
| **WORK LOCATION:** | Schools, recreation centers, runaway shelters, detention centers, and the community |
| **QUOTE:** | "It feels good to be open with teens about many different topics. They should ask questions and explore many issues. They deserve the information. They need to protect themselves." |

### SELF-ASSESSMENT CHECKLIST
### Check It Out!

**I know:**
- [ ] words to describe feelings and emotions
- [ ] examples of folk art

**I know how to:**
- [ ] greet friends
- [ ] respond to greetings
- [ ] write a poem about an emotion
- [ ] design a patchwork quilt on graph paper
- [ ] label objects for a museum display
- [ ] work with place value in whole numbers

# School Rules

13

*I*n this chapter, we will cover the following topics and skills:

**SCHOOL COMMUNICATION**
➤ Rules in my school

**MATH**
➤ Rounding whole numbers

**LANGUAGE ARTS**
➤ Declarative and interrogative sentences

**SOCIAL STUDIES**
➤ Rules in society

**WRITING**
➤ Journal entry: Rules at school

**COMMUNICATION TIP**
➤ Asking about school rules

**CAREER PROFILE**
➤ School security manager

**ASSESSMENT**
➤ Self-assessment checklist

Are there many rules in your school? Why are school rules important?

# That's the Rule

MS. ADAMS: Danny? What are you wearing on your belt?

DANNY: It's my beeper, Ms. Adams.

MS. ADAMS: You know the rule, Danny. Students can't bring beepers to school. You have to leave your beeper at home.

DANNY: But, Ms. Adams, I can't. I use it in my job, and I have to go to work right after school.

MS. ADAMS: I'm sorry, Danny.

DANNY: Can I leave it in my locker?

MS. ADAMS: No, you can't. You have to leave it at home. That's the rule.

## Classmates Exchange

In pairs or small groups, discuss rules in your school.

What can students do?
What can't students do?
What do students have to do?

Share your ideas with the class. Make a complete list of all the rules. As a class, discuss your opinions about the rules in your school.

 **COMMUNICATION TIP**

**Asking About School Rules**

A. Can students *go to their lockers between classes?*

B. No, they can't. That isn't allowed.

A. Can students *go outside during the lunch period?*

B. Yes, they can. That's allowed.

With a classmate, practice conversations about different school rules.

In some schools students have to wear uniforms. What do you think about this rule?

## Classmates Journal

What do you think about the rules in your school? Write your ideas and thoughts in your journal.

Eduardo works after school in a fast-food restaurant. He has to wear a uniform and a hairnet. He has to wash his hands often. He can drink some water or soda on the job, but he can't eat the food. It's a rule of the workplace.

Carina lives in the Fairmont Apartments. She has to park her car in parking space number 43. She can have a small pet, but she can't have a cat or a dog. (She has a bird.) She has to put her trash in the trash room. She can't play loud music after 10:00 P.M. It's a rule of the building.

Omar and his friends play on the school soccer team. Their coach is very strict. They have to practice for two hours every afternoon. They can't miss practice. They have to wear special uniforms. They can't drink, and they can't smoke. It's a team rule.

Rules are everywhere. There are rules in schools, in workplaces, and on city streets. Games have rules. Sports have rules. Families have rules.

What rules are there in your family? in your community? in a game or a sport you know? List the rules below.

| Family | Community | A Game or Sport |
|---|---|---|
| 1 _____ | 1 _____ | 1 _____ |
| 2 _____ | 2 _____ | 2 _____ |
| 3 _____ | 3 _____ | 3 _____ |
| 4 _____ | 4 _____ | 4 _____ |
| 5 _____ | 5 _____ | 5 _____ |

As a class, compare rules in families. Do you and your classmates have different rules at home? Also as a class, make a complete list of the rules in your community.

**MULTICULTURAL AWARENESS/ PUBLISHING PROJECT**

## Game Day!

**CRITICAL THINKING**

## Think About It

Why are rules important in society? Why do we need rules?

Teach your classmates how to play a game or sport from your culture. Teach them the rules of the game and show them how to play it. As a class publishing project, write a handbook of all the games. Draw pictures to illustrate the game rules.

# Language Arts Classmates

## Declarative and Interrogative Sentences with *Can*

A **declarative** sentence gives information. The punctuation mark at the end of a declarative sentence is a **period**.

An **interrogative** sentence asks a question. The punctuation mark at the end of an interrogative sentence is a **question mark**.

**Word order** is different in declarative and interrogative sentences.

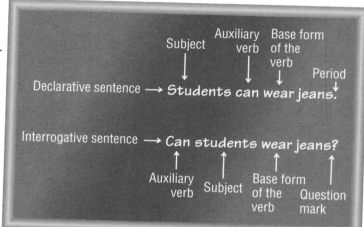

Declarative sentence → **Students can wear jeans.**
- Subject
- Auxiliary verb
- Base form of the verb
- Period

Interrogative sentence → **Can students wear jeans?**
- Auxiliary verb
- Subject
- Base form of the verb
- Question mark

A. What's the sentence?
B. *Maria can speak Spanish.*
A. What kind of sentence is it?
B. It's *a declarative sentence.*
A. What's the punctuation mark?
B. *A period.*
A. Change it to *an interrogative sentence.*
B. Okay. *Can Maria speak Spanish?*

A. What's the sentence?
B. *Can we go outside during lunch today?*
A. What kind of sentence is it?
B. It's *an interrogative sentence.*
A. What's the punctuation mark?
B. *A question mark.*
A. Change it to *a declarative sentence.*
B. Okay. *We can go outside during lunch today.*

---

**Practice conversations about these sentences with a classmate.**

1. She can go to the school dance next Friday.
2. Can Carlos play the violin?
3. Lola can babysit Saturday night.
4. Can Mario type?
5. George and Sonny can play on the soccer team.
6. Can the teacher help us?
7. Can Ms. Lopez sign the hall pass?
8. Jessie can drive a car.
9. Can Sandra and Amy speak Chinese?
10. We can catch the late bus.

We **round off** numbers to make it easier to work with numbers.

When we round off, we increase or decrease a number to a factor of ten: to ones, to tens, to hundreds, to thousands, and so on. We **round down** with numbers less than 5. We **round up** with numbers 5 and greater.

20  21  22  23  24  25  26  27  28  29  30

← round down    round up →

## ROUNDING TO THE NEAREST TEN

A. Round *52* to the nearest ten.
B. The answer is *50*.
A. Why?
B. *52* is close to *50*, so you round down.

A. Round *56* to the nearest ten.
B. The answer is *60*.
A. Why?
B. *56* is close to *60*, so you round up.

Work with a classmate. Give each other 2-digit numbers and practice conversations about rounding up and rounding down.

## ROUNDING TO DIFFERENT PLACES

hundreds place
↓
2,736
round up

A. Round *2,736* to the nearest thousand.
B. The answer is *3,000*.
A. Why?
B. There's a 7 in the hundreds place, so you round up to *3,000*.

tens place
↓
2,736
round down

A. Round *2,736* to the nearest hundred.
B. The answer is *2,700*.
A. Why?
B. There's a 3 in the tens place, so you round down to *2,700*.

ones place
↓
2,736
round up

A. Round *2,736* to the nearest ten.
B. The answer is *2,740*.
A. Why?
B. There's a 6 in the ones place, so you round up to *2,740*.

Work with a classmate. Give each other rounding problems. Practice rounding different 4-digit numbers to the nearest thousand, hundred, and ten.

James Jones
School Security Manager

## School Security Manager

EDUCATION: College coursework
University summer school program

JOB DESCRIPTION: Manage security officers
Check building access and alarm system
Close up building at end of day
Help evacuate building during fire drills

WORK LOCATION: School building

QUOTE: "I see the students move from grade to grade safely. I feel I'm a small part of their well-being."

## ANNOUNCEMENTS

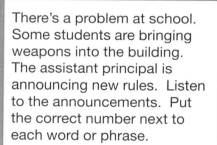

There's a problem at school. Some students are bringing weapons into the building. The assistant principal is announcing new rules. Listen to the announcements. Put the correct number next to each word or phrase.

_____ hall pass

_____ metal detector

_____ clothing

_____ cafeteria

__1__ backpack

_____ 3-ring binder

## SELF-ASSESSMENT CHECKLIST
### Check It Out!

I know:
- ☐ rules at my school
- ☐ rules in society

I know how to:
- ☐ ask about school rules
- ☐ teach a game or sport from my culture
- ☐ identify declarative and interrogative sentences
- ☐ identify punctuation marks: period and question mark
- ☐ round whole numbers

# Registration

*I*n this chapter, we will cover the following topics and skills:

**SCHOOL COMMUNICATION**
➤ Required courses
➤ Electives

**MATH**
➤ Estimating

**SOCIAL STUDIES**
➤ New Year's celebrations and resolutions

**WRITING**
➤ Journal entry: Resolutions

**COMMUNICATION TIP**
➤ Asking for advice on course selection

**CAREER PROFILE**
➤ Guidance counselor

**ASSESSMENT**
➤ Self-assessment checklist

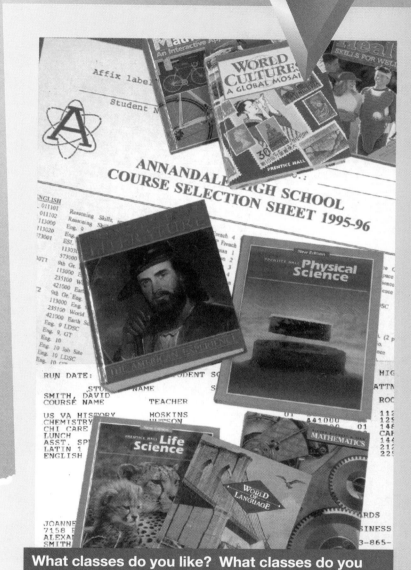

**What classes do you like?  What classes do you want to take?**

# What Classes Are You Going to Take?

DIANA: What classes are you going to take next year?

ERIC: Well, I have to take English, Algebra, World History, Biology, P.E., and Health.

DIANA: And what electives are you going to sign up for?

ERIC: I want to take Keyboarding and Instrumental Music.

DIANA: Keyboarding and Instrumental Music?

ERIC: Yes. I really want to learn to type and to use a computer, and I also want to play in the orchestra.

## Required Courses and Electives

### *Have to* and *Want to*

In all schools there are some classes students *have to* take. These are **required courses**. Some schools call them **core courses**. Other classes are **electives**. Students choose the electives they *want to* take.

## YOUR CLASSES NOW

What required courses are you taking now?

_____

_____

_____

_____

_____

What electives are you taking now?

_____

_____

_____

_____

_____

# Electives in Your School

List some of the electives you can take in your school.

| ART | MUSIC | BUSINESS & TECHNOLOGY | LANGUAGES | OTHER ELECTIVES |
|-----|-------|-----------------------|-----------|-----------------|
| | | | | |
| | | | | |
| | | | | |
| | | | | |
| | | | | |

## YOUR CLASSES NEXT YEAR

What required courses do you have to take next year?

_____

_____

_____

_____

_____

What electives do you want to take next year?

_____

_____

_____

_____

_____

# Classmates Exchange

Have a conversation with a classmate. Ask each other about the required courses and electives you are going to take next year. What are you both going to take? Why?

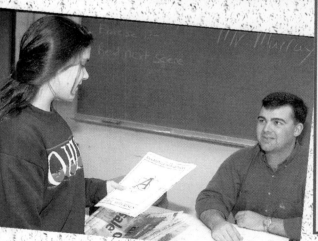

## ✓ COMMUNICATION TIP

**Asking for advice on course selection**

A. Excuse me, *Mr. Carlson.* Can you help me, please?

B. Certainly.

A. I need some help with my course request form. Which courses do I have to take?

B. You have to take English, Social Studies, Math, and Science.

A. And how many electives can I take?

B. You can take two electives.

A. Do you have any suggestions?

B. Well, *Latin* is a very good class. *Drama* is very popular. And *Keyboarding* is very useful.

A. I think I want to take *Woodworking* and *Computer Science.*

# SOCIAL STUDIES
## ClassMates

How do people in your culture celebrate the new year? When do they celebrate? What do they do? Do they eat special foods? Do they sing special songs?

## NEW YEAR'S RESOLUTIONS

Many people make New Year's resolutions. They decide to do something in the new year. Resolutions are often about school, work, family life, or plans for the future. Here are some typical resolutions:

"I'm going to study four hours every day."
"I'm going to save money and buy a car."
"I'm going to help my parents with the housework."
"I'm going to be nice to my sister."

Do people in your culture make resolutions like these? What are some typical resolutions?

### Classmates Journal

Think about your life at school, at home, and in the community. Think about your family and your friends. As you reflect, can you think of any resolutions you want to make? What are you going to do in the future? Write your resolutions in your Classmates Journal.

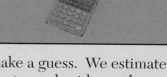

| 58 | rounds to | 60 |
|----|-----------|-----|
| + 31 | → | + 30 |
| 89 | rounds to | 90 |

When we estimate, we make a guess. We estimate numbers to make it easier to work with numbers. One way we estimate is to round each number.

A. How are you going to solve the problem?

B. I'm going to estimate. *58* rounds to *60*, and *31* rounds to *30*.
*60* plus *30* equals *90*. Is that close?

A. Yes. The exact answer is *89*. Your estimate is good.

### Pronunciation Tip

In Speaker B's line, *estimate* is a verb. In Speaker A's last line, *estimate* is the subject. The pronunciations are different. Practice with your teacher.

### Mental Math

*Mental math* is math you do in your head. You don't use a pencil or paper, and you don't use a calculator.

Work with a classmate. Give each other addition problems with 2-digit numbers and practice conversations about estimating. Use *mental math* to estimate the sum. Use a calculator to find the correct sum.

### Math Tip

The word *about* in these word problems is a clue that you estimate to find the answer.

Solve these word problems with estimation. Say how you solve each problem.

1. The school lunchroom serves lunches to 783 students and 112 teachers and staff every day. About how many lunches does the lunchroom serve every day?

| 800 |
|------|
| +100 |
| 900 |

2. There are 763 female students and 824 male students at Lexington High School. About how many students are there at Lexington High?

3. There are 52 computers in the school. Next month, there are going to be 17 more. About how many computers are there going to be in the school next month?

4. Students at Mansfield High can study Latin for 2 years. In Latin I, there are 26 students. In Latin II there are 23 students. About how many students study Latin?

5. At Springfield High, there are 863 ninth graders, 910 tenth graders, 722 eleventh graders, and 808 twelfth graders. About how many students are there?

6. Maura wants to buy a notebook for $2.10, a pen for $1.60, and a bookbag for $9.25. About how much money is she going to spend?

Now make up two original word problems with addition. Give them to a classmate to solve with estimation, and practice conversations.

# ClassMates
## CAREER PROFILE

## Guidance Counselor

Lisa Dyer
Guidance Counselor

EDUCATION: Bachelor of Arts (B.A.) degree in Psychology and Studio Arts

Master in Arts (M.A.) degree in Counseling

JOB DESCRIPTION: Help students select courses

Give school orientations to new students

Help students with problems

WORK LOCATION: Middle school guidance office

QUOTE: "I like to work with students, families, and staff."

## SELF-ASSESSMENT CHECKLIST
## Check It Out!

I know about:
- [ ] required courses at my school
- [ ] elective courses at my school
- [ ] New Year's celebrations and resolutions

I know how to:
- [ ] register for courses at my school
- [ ] ask for advice on course selection
- [ ] solve and talk about word problems with estimation
- [ ] reflect about my life and write about my future plans

# Health and Illness

# 15

*In this chapter, we will cover the following topics and skills:*

**SCHOOL COMMUNICATION**
➤ Health problems

**MATH**
➤ Word problems in the past tense

**WRITING**
➤ Journal entry: A day when I felt terrible

**SOCIAL STUDIES**
➤ Martial arts from Asia

**COMMUNICATION TIP**
➤ Describing illness to the school nurse

**CAREER PROFILE**
➤ School nurse

**ASSESSMENT**
➤ Self-assessment checklist

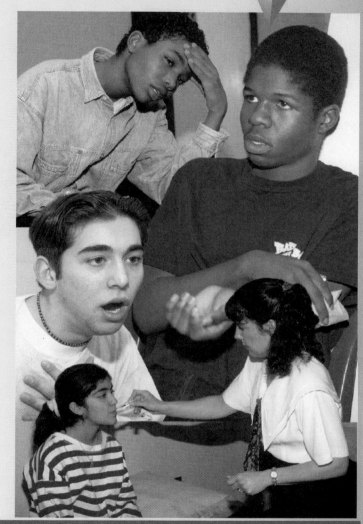

**What problems do you think these students have?**

# I Feel Terrible!

FREDDY: Excuse me. *Mrs. Franklin?*

MRS. FRANKLIN: Hello, *Freddy.* What can I do for you?

FREDDY: I feel terrible.

MRS. FRANKLIN: What seems to be the problem?

FREDDY: *My head hurts.*

With a classmate, practice conversations about illnesses.

My stomach hurts.

My back hurts.

My tooth hurts.

My ear hurts.

I have a bad cough.

I have a sore throat.

I have a stiff neck.

I have a bad cold.

 *Ways to Say It!*

My stomach hurts. = I have a stomachache.

My head hurts. = I have a headache.

My back hurts. = I have a backache.

My tooth hurts. = I have a toothache.

My ear hurts. = I have an earache.

I have a rash.

I have cramps.

I have the chills.

I feel nauseous.

I feel faint.

I feel dizzy.

I'm wheezing.

I'm congested.

## Ways to Say It

I feel nauseous. = I feel like I'm going to throw up.

I feel faint. = I feel like I'm going to faint.

## ✔ COMMUNICATION TIP

**Describing illness to the school nurse**

MRS. FRANKLIN: What's the matter?

MARY: I have a stomachache.

MRS. FRANKLIN: What did you eat this morning?

MARY: I ate *cold pizza*, and I drank *diet soda*.

MRS. FRANKLIN: I see.

You have a stomachache! You're at the nurse's office. Practice the conversation with a classmate. Use different food and drink items.

# What Did You Do?

| | |
|---|---|
| JOSEPH: | Excuse me, Mrs. Franklin. |
| MRS. FRANKLIN: | Yes? |
| JOSEPH: | I got hurt. |
| MRS. FRANKLIN: | What did you do? |
| JOSEPH: | *I twisted my ankle.* |

I twisted my ankle.

I sprained my wrist.

I dislocated my shoulder.

I scratched my eye.

I scraped my knee.

I bruised my arm.

I burned my hand.

I cut my finger.

## Classmates Journal

Describe a day when you felt terrible. How did you feel? Why? What did you do? Did you go to school? Who helped you? Write about that day in your Classmates Journal.

## What Do You Think?

In pairs or small groups, discuss how students in your school use the nurse's office. What are good reasons to go to the nurse's office? What does the nurse do for different health problems?

# JEFFERSON HIGH SCHOOL TIMES

Vol. 22  No. 6 | January

## FOOTBALL TEAM KEEPS NURSE'S OFFICE BUSY

by Rocky Chen

Coach Bryant and the varsity football team ____had____ [1] big problems last weekend. The problems started at practice on Friday afternoon.

Field goal kicker Hector Pineda _____ [2] (practice) well for the first 10 minutes. Suddenly, Hector _____ [3] (sit) down on the field and _____ [4] (shout) to the coach, "Help! I just _____ [5] (twist) my ankle!" The coach and trainers _____ [6] (help) Hector off the field and into the nurse's office.

About 5 minutes later, Quarterback John Perry _____ [7] (throw) the ball to another player and _____ [8] (sprain) his wrist. He _____ [9] (walk) slowly to the nurse's office.

Fullback Choi Yung _____ [10] (arrive) twenty minutes late for practice. He _____ [11] (say), "I'm nauseous." He _____ [12] (drink) a lot of water, and then he _____ [13] (throw) up. He _____ [14] (go) to the nurse's office, too.

A few minutes later, Assistant Coach Amy Vogel _____ [15] (scratch) her eye. She _____ [16] (leave) practice and _____ [17] (wait) in line at the nurse's office.

Believe it or not, Coach Bryant's team _____ [18] (play) very well at the game on Saturday. The final score: Jefferson 7, Weston 6! Congratulations, team! And we hope you all feel better soon!

| go | — | went |
|------|---|-------|
| have | — | had |
| leave | — | left |
| say | — | said |
| throw | — | threw |

# ClassMates

These kids aren't fighting. They're practicing their favorite sport, **Tae Kwon Do**. Tae Kwon Do is one of the martial arts. Many people like to do this because it's good exercise. Other people do this because it's good for concentration or for self-defense. The martial arts come from countries in Asia.

## MARTIAL ARTS

| Martial arts with kicking and hitting | Martial arts without kicking and hitting |
| --- | --- |

**Karate** comes from Japan.

**Tae Kwon Do** comes from Korea.

**Kung Fu** comes from China.

**Judo** comes from Japan.

## USING A GRAPHIC ORGANIZER

Use a Venn diagram to compare two of the martial arts. Show how they are the same and how they are different.

## ? What Do You Think?

Do you know any of the martial arts? Which one interests you? Why? Do you think it's a good idea to practice martial arts? Where can you learn martial arts in your community?

The tennis team drank 20 bottles of water. The soccer team drank 35 bottles of water. How many bottles of water did the teams drink?

A. How did you solve the problem?
B. I added.
A. What did you add?
B. I added *20* and *35*.
A. What's the sum?
B. *55*.
A. *So how many bottles of water did the teams drink?*
B. *The teams drank 55 bottles of water.*

Bakersfield High School scored 26 points at last Friday's football game. Reed High School scored 17 points. How many more points did Bakersfield High score?

A. How did you solve the problem?
B. I subtracted.
A. What did you subtract?
B. I subtracted *17* from *26*.
A. What's the difference?
B. *9.*
A. *So how many more points did Bakersfield High score?*
B. *Bakersfield High scored 9 more points than Reed High.*

Solve these word problems. Then practice conversations about these problems with a classmate.

1. Forty-six female students and 62 male students played on school sports teams last year. How many students played on school teams last year?

2. There are 35 students in Mr. Garza's Computer Science class. 30 students finished their projects yesterday. How many students didn't finish their projects?

3. The cafeteria served 145 hamburgers yesterday. They served 70 hamburgers during the 1st lunch period. How many hamburgers did they serve during the 2nd lunch period?

4. Louis worked 10 hours last week and 12 hours this week. How many hours did Louis work in the last two weeks?

5. Mr. Sao asked 24 females and 35 males to try out for the track team. How many students did Mr. Sao ask to try out?

6. On a test with 100 questions, Sally answered 93 correctly. How many questions did Sally answer incorrectly?

7. Miss Van, the guidance counselor, helped 75 students last month. She helped 32 male students. How many female students did she help?

8. Students moved 125 chairs from Room 122 and 120 chairs from Room 124 into the auditorium. How many chairs did the students move into the auditorium?

**Now make up two original word problems, one with addition and one with subtraction. Give them to a classmate and practice conversations.**

## School Nurse

Heidi H. Capelli, R.N.
School Nurse

EDUCATION: Bachelor of Science (B.S.) degree in Nursing.

JOB DESCRIPTION: Treat students' minor injuries

Keep medical records of all students

Give prescription medicines

Look for health risks around the school

WORK LOCATION: Nurse's office of a school

QUOTE: "I like to help people with their medical problems. I enjoy students, and I like to help them learn about healthy living."

---

**SELF-ASSESSMENT CHECKLIST**

## Check It Out!

I know about:
- ☐ health problems
- ☐ martial arts

I know how to:
- ☐ describe symptoms, illnesses, and injuries to the school nurse
- ☐ use a Venn diagram to compare and contrast
- ☐ solve and talk about word problems in the past tense
- ☐ write about a day when I felt terrible

# Student Responsibilities

*I*n this chapter, we will cover the following topics and skills:

**SCHOOL COMMUNICATION**
➤ Student responsibilities
➤ Detention
➤ Hall passes
➤ Study habits

**MATH**
➤ Word problems in the past tense

**WRITING**
➤ Journal entry: About homework

**LANGUAGE ARTS**
➤ Interrogative sentences in the past tense

**LITERATURE**
➤ Homework by Russell Hoban

**SOCIAL STUDIES**
➤ Time in our lives

**COMMUNICATION TIP**
➤ Asking for a hall pass

**CAREER PROFILE**
➤ Assistant principal

**ASSESSMENT**
➤ Self-assessment checklist

What are some responsibilities students have?
Which responsibilities are the most important?

# I forgot to Bring It to Class

MRS. LEE: Armando, did you do your homework last night?

ARMANDO: No, I didn't, Mrs. Lee. I worked late again last night. I'm sorry.

MRS. LEE: Did you finish your research project?

ARMANDO: Yes, I did, but I forgot to bring it to class.

MRS. LEE: Well, where is it?

ARMANDO: It's in my locker.

MRS. LEE: Go to your locker and get your research project, Armando. I'm going to write you a hall pass.

ARMANDO: Thank you, Mrs. Lee.

MRS. LEE: You're welcome, Armando. And next time, be responsible. Don't forget your assignments.

ARMANDO: Yes, ma'am.

## Student Responsibilities

In pairs or in small groups, make a list of student responsibilities.

Students have to come to class on time.

Students have to bring their books and supplies to class.

Students have to do their homework.

_____

_____

_____

**Now share your list with the class and make a complete list of student responsibilities.**

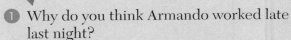

## Think About It!

1. Why do you think Armando worked late last night?
2. Why do you think Armando works?
3. Do you think it's difficult to go to school and work at the same time?
4. Do you work? If you work, answer these questions:
   How many hours a week do you work?
   When do you work?
   When do you do homework?
   When do you sleep?
   Do you have time to do everything?

## Classmates Exchange

A. *Mr. Barton* is upset with me.
B. Why?
A. I didn't *come to class on time*.

Practice the conversation with a classmate. Then practice new conversations. Use the student responsibilities from your list above.

# Detention

Students cannot
- leave the school grounds during the school day.
- bring electronic equipment to school.
- smoke in the building.
- use foul language.

A. What did you do to get detention?
B. I left the school grounds during lunch. What did YOU do?
A. I brought a beeper to school. What did Susanna do?
B. She smoked a cigarette in the bathroom. What did Jake do?
A. He used foul language with the gym teacher.

## Classmates Exchange

With a classmate, think of four other school rules. Then create a conversation: You and your classmate served detention today! Why? What did you do? What did other students in the detention room do? Practice your conversation and present it to the class. (Remember: Don't talk in the detention room! Have your conversation in the hallway before or after detention.)

## SERVING DETENTION

Students sometimes get **detention** when they break classroom rules or school rules. They **serve detention** after school or during lunch. They have to sit in the **detention room** or **detention hall**. They can't talk with each other, and they can't get up and move around. They have to sit and do their assignments.

## ✓ COMMUNICATION TIP

### Asking for a Hall Pass

A. Excuse me, *Mrs. Lee.* May I have a hall pass? *I have an appointment with my guidance counselor.*
B. Okay. Here you are.

**Practice with a classmate. Ask for a hall pass.**

## HALL PASS

Name _____   Date _____
                Time _____

Destination:
- ☐ Library
- ☐ Nurse's office
- ☐ Main office
- ☐ Guidance office
- ☐ Restroom

Teacher's signature

_____

## Homework

### by Russell Hoban

Homework sits on top of Sunday, squashing Sunday flat.
Homework has the smell of Monday, homework's very fat.
Heavy books and piles of paper, answers I don't know.
Sunday evening's almost finished, now I'm going to go
Do my homework in the kitchen.  Maybe just a snack,
Then I'll sit right down and start as soon as I run back
For some chocolate sandwich cookies.  Then I'll really do
All that homework in a minute.  First I'll see what new
Show they've got on television in the living room.
Everybody's laughing there, but misery and gloom
And a full refrigerator are where I am at.
I'll just have another sandwich.  Homework's very fat.

## THE WRITER'S CRAFT

### Personification

Writers use personification to give human characteristics, such as movement and life, to nonhuman things.  For example, in Russell Hoban's poem, homework *sits*.  What other examples of personification can you find in "*Homework*"?

## Classmates Journal

How do you feel about homework?  Do you like to do homework?  Why do teachers give homework?  Do your teachers give a lot of homework?  Write your ideas in your journal.

## Homework Habits Checklist

Check the homework habits that describe you.  Then compare your homework habits with your classmates.

- [ ] I write my homework assignments in an assignment book.
- [ ] I have a special time for homework every day.
- [ ] I read every day.
- [ ] I study in a quiet place.
- [ ] I listen to music and do homework at the same time.
- [ ] I watch TV and do homework at the same time.
- [ ] Somebody at home checks my homework.
- [ ] I study for tests.
- [ ] I use a dictionary to find new words.
- [ ] I use the library.

- [ ] I work on projects for many days.
- [ ] I do projects at the last minute.
- [ ] I do my homework at a desk or table.
- [ ] I do my homework on the floor.
- [ ] I do my homework on my bed.
- [ ] I have paper, pens, and pencils at home.

### ART CONNECTION

### Create a Poster

As a class, make a list of the Top Ten Homework Habits.  Create posters about your list.  Draw pictures to illustrate your ideas.  Put up the posters in your classroom and in the hall.

In the movie *Safety Last*, the famous actor Harold Lloyd has a problem with time. He doesn't have enough time in his day, so he tries to stop the clock.

In the old days, more people lived on farms. They looked at time in a different way. Nature divided the year into seasons. The sun came up, and work began. The sun went down, and work ended. People didn't look at watches or clocks all day.

Later, people moved to cities. They worked in factories. They punched time clocks at their workplaces. Time clocks measured hours, minutes, and seconds. People looked at time in a new way, and it changed their lives.

Today, time is very important in our society. People look at clocks all the time. Digital watches measure time in fractions of seconds. People use appointment calendars. Their schedules are busy. They're always in a hurry. They don't want to be late. They don't want to lose time.

## Classmates Exchange

Write out your daily schedule. List everything you do during the day. Be exact! Use hours and minutes. Share your schedule with a classmate. How are your schedules the same? How are they different?

## Time in Different Cultures

In different parts of the world, people look at time in different ways. In some places, trains and buses always run on schedule. In some places, trains and buses are always late. In other places, there aren't any schedules for trains or buses. In some countries, people arrive at parties on time. In other countries, they arrive early or late. Find out about time in different cultures. Interview three people from different countries. Ask these questions and make up your own questions. Take notes during your interviews.

Do people arrive at school on time?
Do people arrive at work on time?
Do people arrive at appointments on time?
Do people arrive at parties on time?
Do trains and buses run on schedule?
Do movies begin on time?
Do sports events begin on time?
Do workplaces use time clocks or timesheets?

Choose one of the interviews. Use your notes and write a report about time in that culture. Then make an oral presentation to the class.

# Word Problems in the Past Tense (Multiplication and Division)

The gymnastics team practiced for 12 hours last week. They practiced for equal amounts of time on 4 afternoons. How many hours did they practice each afternoon?

A. How did you solve the problem?
B. I divided.
A. What did you divide?
B. { I divided 4 into 12. }
{ I divided 12 by 4. }
A. What's the quotient?
B. 3.
A. So *how many hours did they practice each afternoon?*
B. *They practiced 3 hours each afternoon.*

There are 40 students in the International Club. Each student invited 2 people to an international dinner. How many people did the students invite?

A. How did you solve the problem?
B. I multiplied.
A. What did you multiply?
B. I multiplied *40* and *2*.
A. What's the product?
B. *80*.
A. So *how many people did the students invite?*
B. *They invited 80 people.*

① Marilyn read at the library for 4 hours each day on Monday, Tuesday, Wednesday, and Thursday. How many hours did she read last week?

② Ms. Ahmed's History class had a busy day yesterday. The 35 students worked in groups. Five students worked together in each group. How many groups did Ms. Ahmed have?

③ Mr. Stewart's writing class worked on the computer yesterday. The 28 students worked in pairs, and each pair had a computer. How many computers did the class share?

④ On Earth Day, 24 students in the Environmental Club each planted 3 trees in the vacant lot next to the school. How many trees did they plant?

⑤ Mrs. Lane changed the desks again! She put the 32 desks into groups of 4. How many groups did she make?

⑥ The cafeteria workers ordered 2 hot dogs for every student in the school. There are 220 students. How many hot dogs did the cafeteria workers order?

⑦ Mr. Gordon bought 8 packages of composition notebooks. Ten composition notebooks are in each package. How many notebooks did Mr. Gordon buy?

⑧ The 40 students on the Debate Team practiced in teams of 4. How many groups did they make?

Now make up two original word problems, one with multiplication and one with division. Give them to a classmate and practice conversations.

# Language Arts ClassMates

One type of interrogative sentence is the **Yes/No question**.

A Yes/No question begins with an auxiliary verb.

The answer to a Yes/No question is affirmative (Yes) or negative (No).

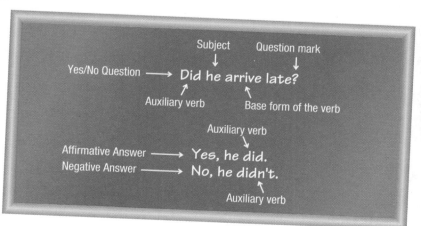

Subject — Question mark

Yes/No Question → **Did he arrive late?**

Auxiliary verb — Base form of the verb

Auxiliary verb

Affirmative Answer → **Yes, he did.**
Negative Answer → **No, he didn't.**

Auxiliary verb

A. What's the interrogative sentence?
B. *Did he miss the school bus?*
A. What's the auxiliary verb?
B. *Did.*
A. What's the base form of the verb?
B. *Miss.*
A. What's the answer to the question?
B. *Yes, he did.*

Read the story. Answer the questions. Then practice conversations about the interrogative sentences with a classmate.

### "Roger and His Terrible Morning"

Roger had a bad morning yesterday. He got up late, missed the school bus, and walked to school. He arrived late for school, went to the principal's office, and got a hall pass. He went to his locker to get his books, but he forgot his locker combination. He went to his first period class without his books. His teacher asked for the homework. His teacher looked at Roger's assignment and said, "I'm sorry, Roger. You did the wrong assignment. I assigned page 67, but you did page 76." Roger had a big headache!

1. Did Roger have a bad morning yesterday?
2. Did he get up late?
3. Did he take the school bus to school?
4. Did he arrive late for school?
5. Did he go to the guidance counselor's office?
6. Did he get a hall pass?
7. Did he get his books from his locker?
8. Did Roger's teacher assign page 76?
9. Did Roger do the correct homework assignment?
10. Did Roger have a headache yesterday morning?

## Assistant Principal

Teresa Bratt
Assistant Principal

EDUCATION: Bachelor of Arts (B.A.) degree in French Literature

Master of Arts in Teaching (M.A.T.) degree

Coursework in French, linguistics, ESL Methodology, and School Administration

JOB DESCRIPTION: Supervise students' behavior, attendance, and activities

Work with teachers on curricula

Help the principal with the school so that everything runs smoothly and efficiently

WORK LOCATION: Main office of a high school

QUOTE: "I enjoy teenagers."

### SELF-ASSESSMENT CHECKLIST

## ✓ Check It Out!

**I know about:**

- ☐ student responsibilities at my school
- ☐ reasons for getting detention
- ☐ hall passes
- ☐ homework habits
- ☐ the importance of time in our society
- ☐ time in different cultures

**I know how to:**

- ☐ ask for a hall pass
- ☐ evaluate my study habits
- ☐ write my daily schedule
- ☐ interview people about cultural differences in how they look at time
- ☐ solve and talk about word problems in the past tense
- ☐ identify Yes/No questions
- ☐ give short answers to Yes/No questions

# Diversity in
# School

*In* this chapter, we will cover the following topics and skills:

**SCHOOL COMMUNICATION**
➤ Cultural differences
➤ Holidays in different cultures

**MATH**
➤ Word problems in the past tense with mixed operations

**WRITING**
➤ The Writing Process: Pre-writing, Organizing ideas, Writing a first draft, Revising, Writing a final copy

**SOCIAL STUDIES**
➤ Immigration

**LITERATURE**
➤ Our Escape by Shukri Sindi

**COMMUNICATION TIP**
➤ Explaining an absence for a holiday observance

**CAREER PROFILE**
➤ ESL teacher

**ASSESSMENT**
➤ Self-assessment checklist

What is diversity? How do you think these students are different? How do you think they are the same? Is there diversity in your school?

125

# Differences

STEVE: Hey, Ahmad. Where were you yesterday? Were you sick?

AHMAD: No, I wasn't. I was at home all day. It was Idul-Fitr—the holiday we celebrate after Ramadan. All my relatives were at my house. My aunts and uncles were there. All my cousins were there. My grandparents were there. And my great grandmother was there. We ate lots of food, and we stayed up late.

STEVE: You missed a science quiz.

AHMAD: I did?

STEVE: Yeah. And we also had a quiz in math. You know what I think, Ahmad?

AHMAD: What?

STEVE: I think the teachers didn't know about your holiday.

AHMAD: You're probably right. I'm going to talk to them.

## Think About It

Ahmad missed two quizzes yesterday. He was at home with his family to celebrate a holiday. In your opinion, was it okay for Ahmad to stay at home yesterday? Was it okay for Ahmad's teachers to give quizzes on his holiday? Do your teachers know your holidays?

## Act It Out!

**ROLE PLAY**

Ahmad is talking to his science teacher. He's explaining his absence. With a classmate, practice a conversation between them and perform it for the class.

## Writing  A Holiday Memory

THE WRITING PROCESS

- Pre-writing
- Organizing ideas
- Writing a first draft
- Revising
- Writing a final copy

Write about a holiday in your past.

BRAINSTORM    What was the holiday? When was it? How old were you? Where did you celebrate the holiday? Who was with you? How did you celebrate? Why was this holiday special? Write your ideas in words and phrases.

ORGANIZE YOUR IDEAS    Look at your notes. What are you going to write about first? second? third? Organize your ideas.

WRITE A FIRST DRAFT    Write about the details of your holiday. Use this title: "A Holiday Memory".

REVISE    Give your first draft to your teacher. Have a conference with your teacher to discuss the first draft. Talk about your teacher's suggestions for corrections and revisions.

WRITE A FINAL COPY    Write a final copy, and hand it in to your teacher. Put together all your classmates' holiday memories in a book. Make copies for every student.

# Holidays Around the World

Do a research project about a holiday in another culture.

**CHOOSE A TOPIC:** Interview somebody from another culture or country. Ask about an important holiday. Take notes as the person describes the holiday.

**GO TO THE LIBRARY:** At the library, find information about the culture and the holiday in encyclopedias, books, or magazines. What is the meaning of the holiday? What do people do on the holiday? Where do they celebrate? Do they wear special clothes? What do they eat? Do they sing or dance?

**TAKE NOTES:** Write the information on index cards. Also, put your notes from the interview on index cards. Use a separate index card for each piece of information. On each card, write the **source** of the information - the title of the book or article, or the name of the person you interviewed.

**ORGANIZE YOUR NOTES:** Look at all your index cards. Make piles of cards for information that goes together. Then put the cards in order. What are you going to write about first? second? third?

**WRITE A FIRST DRAFT:** Write a paper about the holiday. Give your paper a title.

**REVISE:** Ask a classmate to read your first draft. What questions or suggestions does your classmate have? Discuss them with your classmate. Then revise your first draft.

**WRITE A FINAL COPY:** Write your final copy in ink, or type it on a computer if you can. Indent each paragraph. Check all your punctuation.

**ORAL PRESENTATION:** Stand in front of the class and tell your classmates about the holiday. Don't read from your paper. After your presentation, answer your classmates' questions.

**PUBLISH YOUR WORK:** As a class, put all the research papers together to make a book. Give the book a title. Present the book to the school librarian.

## COMMUNICATION TIP

**Explaining an absence for a holiday observance**

A. *Amania,* where were you yesterday?
B. I was at the *mosque.*
A. Oh. Was it some sort of holiday?
B. Yes. It was *a religious celebration.*

## Immigration

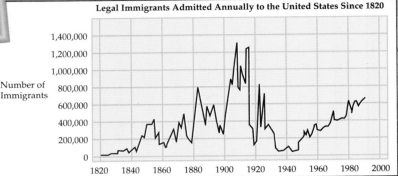

Legal Immigrants Admitted Annually to the United States Since 1820

People immigrate to another country for many different reasons. Some people immigrate because there is fighting in their country. Many people immigrate because they don't have freedom in their country. Other people immigrate because they want to be with their families. Some people immigrate because they want better opportunities for work and education.

How does it feel to immigrate? Many **immigrants** have mixed feelings. They are happy and sad at the same time. They are sad to leave their homes and families and friends. They are happy to be in a new country. But the new country is so different. It's hard to understand the language, the people, and the culture.

The United States is a nation of immigrants. Before 1965, most immigrants to the United States were from Europe. After that year, more immigrants began to arrive from other parts of the world. Today, most immigrants are from Mexico, the Philippines, Haiti, South Korea, China, the Dominican Republic, India, Vietnam, Jamaica, and Cuba.

Many people come to the United States as **refugees**. They leave their countries to escape war and political problems. Refugees come from all over the world – from Vietnam, from Somalia, from Bosnia, and from other countries.

There are also many **undocumented aliens** in the United States. They enter without permission. Many of them leave their countries because of war and political problems. Other aliens come to make a better life for their families. They often work very hard to help family members in the United States and back home.

The line graph shows the number of legal immigrants to the United States since 1820. About how many immigrants arrived in 1930? in 1960?

# Voters Approve Proposition 187

### Services to immigrants may be cut

SACRAMENTO: Voters in California approved Proposition 187 in yesterday's election. They

## ANTI-IMMIGRANT SENTIMENT

Many people in the United States think immigration is a problem. They say immigrants take jobs from American citizens. They say education and other help for immigrants is expensive. They say that people from so many cultures and languages are a problem.

Do you hear *anti-immigrant sentiment* in school? in the community? on the news? What do you hear? How does this make you feel? What can you do about this problem? Discuss these questions in pairs or small groups. Then, share your ideas as a class. (Invite your principal, assistant principal, and guidance counselors to your class discussion.)

## Our Escape

by Shukri Sindi

*My Immigration Story* by Shukri Sindi

In March 1991, the Gulf War stopped. We had to leave our land in the north. The soldiers used many kinds of weapons against us – bombs, guns, tanks, helicopters, and even chemical weapons. We did not have time to pack our bags. We escaped without warm clothes or food. I didn't even wear my shoes.

I didn't know where we were going, but I knew we were going to a safe place. However, on the way, many families got separated. People lost track of each other. Children got lost, old people stayed behind because they could not walk, and young men went to fight the soldiers.

Finally, we escaped to the mountains of Turkey. We walked for three days and three nights and didn't stop. We stayed in Turkey for about three years. Then we came to this land of freedom—the United States.

Shukri Sindi was born in Kurdistan, a region in the northern part of Iraq. After the Gulf War, he fled with his family to Turkey. He lived in a refugee camp there for 2 1/2 years. Now he lives in Virginia with his parents and ten brothers and sisters. Shukri wants to study art in college. After that, he wants to go back to Iraq to work for peace.

### Your Immigration Story

Did you or someone in your family immigrate to this country? When? How? From what country? What was the reason? What happened during the journey? Tell a personal immigration story. Illustrate your story with pictures. Show each major event in the immigration story.

# INTERROGATIVE SENTENCES IN THE PAST TENSE: WH- Questions with *was* and *were*

One kind of interrogative sentence is the **WH- question.** A WH- question begins with a WH- word—Who, What, Where, When, Why, Who, How long, How many. The answer to a WH- question is new information.

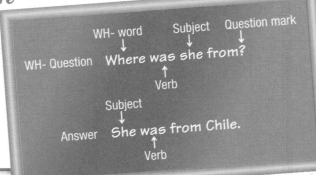

WH- Question    WH- word    Subject    Question mark
**Where was she from?**
Verb

Answer    Subject
**She was from Chile.**
Verb

A. What's the interrogative sentence?
B. *Who was Gabriela Mistral?*
A. What's the WH- word?
B. *Who.*
A. What's the verb?
B. *Was.*
A. What's the subject?
B. *Gabriela Mistral.*
A. What's the answer to the question?
B. *Gabriela Mistral was a famous poet.*

Gabriela Mistral (1889-1957) was a famous poet and teacher. She was a schoolteacher in Chile and in the United States. In 1954, she was the first Latin American and the first woman to win the Nobel Prize for literature.

Gabriela Mistral was born Lucila Godoy Alcayaga in 1889 in Vicuña, Chile. Her childhood was difficult. Her family was poor, and she didn't go to school until she was nine years old. She was very shy, but she was a very good student.

Her first teaching job was in 1905 in Chile. Her students were very poor, and she remembered her difficult life as a young girl. She wanted all students to get a good education.

She wrote her thoughts in poetry. At this time her pen name became Gabriela Mistral to honor her favorite writers.

Her best known books are *Desolation, Tenderness, Felling Trees,* and *Wine Press.* Gabriela Mistral died in 1957 in New York.

Read the story about the famous poet Gabriela Mistral. Answer the questions. Then practice conversations about the interrogative sentences with a classmate.

1. Who was Gabriela Mistral?
2. Where was she a schoolteacher?
3. In what year was she the winner of the Nobel Prize for literature?
4. Where was Gabriela Mistral born?
5. When was she born?
6. What was her real name?
7. How was her childhood?
8. How old was she when she went to school for the first time?
9. When was her first teaching job?
10. What were the names of some of her books?
11. Where was Gabriela Mistral when she died?

There are 38 students in Mr. Green's Music class. Last Monday, 5 students were absent. How many students were present?

A. How did you solve the problem?
B. *I subtracted.*
A. What did you *subtract*?
B. *I subtracted 5 from 38.*
A. *So how many students were present?*
B. *33 students were present.*

During warm-up exercises for the track team, Coach Ryan made 4 groups out of 48 track team members. How many teammates were there in each group?

A. How did you solve the problem?
B. *I divided.*
A. What did you *divide*?
B. *I divided 4 into 48.*
A. *So how many teammates were there in each group?*
B. *There were 12 teammates in each group.*

① Miss Decker's class of 32 students is very diverse. 23 students were born in Haiti, Cuba, China, Korea, or Mexico. The rest were born in Peru. How many were born in Peru?

② There were 30 students in Mrs. Jordan's English class last year. When they worked in groups, 6 students worked in each group. How many groups were there?

③ Roberto earned $4.00 an hour for babysitting last weekend. He babysat for 7 hours. How much money did he earn?

④ At the school assembly, there were 124 ninth graders, 138 tenth graders, 115 eleventh graders, and 142 twelfth graders. How many students were at the assembly?

⑤ On a test of 50 questions, Kerry got 45 correct. How many of Kerry's answers were incorrect?

⑥ The Palmer High School basketball team scored 15 points in each of the 4 quarters of the game. What was the Palmer team's score?

⑦ The guidance counselor registered 10 new students on Monday, 7 on Tuesday, and 8 on Wednesday. How many new students were there altogether?

⑧ At Towson High School last year, 86 female students and 73 male students spoke two languages. How many students at Towson High were bilingual?

**Now make up four original problems, one for each operation – addition, subtraction, multiplication, and division. Give the problems to a classmate and practice conversations.**

## ESL Teacher

Van Nga Pham Vu
ESL Teacher

EDUCATION: Bachelor of Arts (B.A) degree in English

Bachelor of Science (B.S.) degree in Institutional Management

Master of Arts (M.A.) degree in English Linguistics

JOB DESCRIPTION: Help students with reading, writing, speaking, and listening

Help prepare students for mainstream classes

Help students get ready for jobs or for college

WORK LOCATION: High school

QUOTE: "Teaching is an important job. I understand my students very well. I was an ESL student a few years ago."

## SELF-ASSESSMENT CHECKLIST

## Check It Out!

**I know about:**
- ☐ holidays in different cultures
- ☐ reasons people immigrate
- ☐ immigrants, refugees, and undocumented aliens
- ☐ anti-immigrant sentiment

**I know how to:**
- ☐ write about a holiday in the past
- ☐ interview people about holidays in their culture
- ☐ do a research project
  - ☐ find information in encyclopedias, books, and magazines
  - ☐ take notes on index cards
  - ☐ organize information
  - ☐ write a first draft
  - ☐ have a writing conference with a classmate
  - ☐ revise a first draft
  - ☐ write a final copy
  - ☐ give an oral presentation
- ☐ explain an absence for a holiday observance
- ☐ tell a personal immigration story
- ☐ identify WH- questions
- ☐ answer WH- questions based on a reading
- ☐ solve and talk about word problems in the past tense

# Scripts for Listening Exercises

## Page 5

Listen to the question. Circle the best answer.

1. What's your address?
2. What's your name?
3. What country are you from?
4. What's your telephone number?
5. What's your social security number?
6. What's your zip code?

## Page 15

Listen and write the number on the correct line.

1. My bookbag is in the classroom.
2. I need my calculator for Math class.
3. May I borrow an eraser?
4. Where's your assignment book?
5. My markers are in my pencil case.
6. Take out a piece of paper.
7. His pencils are in his pencil case.
8. Where's your ruler?

## Page 25

Listen and circle the letter of the word you hear.

1. I'm going to my first period class.
2. My address is 6 Park Road.
3. It's two o'clock.
4. It's two-oh-five.
5. That calculator is seven dollars.
6. This notebook is four dollars and fifty cents.
7. My English class is in room 32.
8. It's three dollars and thirty cents.
9. Lunch is at twelve-oh-five.
10. She's in the eleventh grade.

## Page 33

Listen and write the number under the correct picture.

1. She's doing her homework on the computer.
2. Tom's sharpening his pencil.
3. The teacher is reading to the class.
4. Mike's writing on the board.
5. They're raising their hands.
6. She's using a calculator.
7. Gina's erasing the board.
8. They're handing in their papers.

## Page 44

Mr. Green's science classes are in different rooms today. Listen and write the correct room number for each period.

May I have your attention, please. Because of the accident in Mr. Green's chemistry lab, Mr. Green's classes are meeting in the following rooms today.

Mr. Green's first period Chemistry class is in Room 210 today.

Mr. Green's second period Physics class is in Room 206.

The third period Biology class is in Room 128.

The fourth period Chemistry class is in Room 214.

The fifth period General Science class is in Room 113.

Mr. Green's sixth period study hall is in Room 218 today.

By the way, Mr. Green is okay. He's resting at home. Have a good day.

## Page 50

Listen and circle the number you hear.

1. Eight
2. Eleven
3. Twenty-two
4. Forty-five
5. One hundred and five
6. Eighty-six

## Page 56

Listen and write the number under the correct picture.

1. Turn to page 27 in your History book.
2. Sound of pencil being sharpened
3. Your attention, please. Here are today's announcements.
4. I'm answering the question.
5. Sound of a computer being used
6. Sound of someone writing with chalk on a board

## Page 58

Write and solve the addition problems you hear.

1. What's two plus eight?
2. How much is ten plus three?
3. Six plus four equals . . .
4. Add five and nine.
5. What's the sum of thirteen and fifteen?
6. How much does twenty-seven plus eleven equal?

## Page 66

Write and solve the subtraction problems you hear.

1. What's seven minus two?
2. Thirteen minus ten equals . . .
3. How much is fifteen minus five?
4. How much does twenty-nine minus ten equal?
5. Take six from eighteen.
6. What's the difference between sixteen and five?

## Page 74

Write and solve the multiplication problems you hear.

1. What's nine times four?
2. Six times five equals . . .
3. How much is four times two?
4. What's the product of five times nine?
5. Find the product of three times seven.
6. Multiply ten times eight.

## Page 82

Write and solve the division problems you hear.

1. What's thirty-six divided by nine?
2. How much does sixty divided by six equal?
3. Divide thirty by five.
4. How much is twenty-seven divided by three?
5. Divide five into fifty.
6. Eighty-one divided by nine equals . . .

## Page 95

Listen and circle the correct number.

1. The 4 is in the ones place.
2. The 6 is in the tens place.
3. The 5 is in the hundreds place.
4. The 7 is in the tens place.
5. The value of the 6 is 600.
6. The value of the 7 is 7,000.
7. The value of the 1 is 10.
8. The value of the 4 is 4.

## Page 102

There's a problem at school. Some students are bringing weapons into the building. The assistant principal is announcing new rules. Listen to the announcements. Put the correct number next to each word or phrase.

Attention, all students. Attention, please. We are all very concerned about safety in our school. As you know, some students are bringing knives and other weapons into the building. This can't continue. For this reason, we have six new rules effective Monday morning.

Rule #1: Students cannot have backpacks in the halls or classrooms.

Rule #2: Students have to carry all their notes and papers in a 3-ring binder.

Rule #3: Starting Monday, students have to pass through a metal detector to enter the school.

Rule #4: Students cannot leave the cafeteria during their lunch period.

Rule #5: Students cannot wear baggy pants or jackets to school.

Rule #6: Students have to have a hall pass to leave classrooms during class time.

Remember, these rules are for your safety. Have a pleasant weekend, everybody.

# Index